AF482136

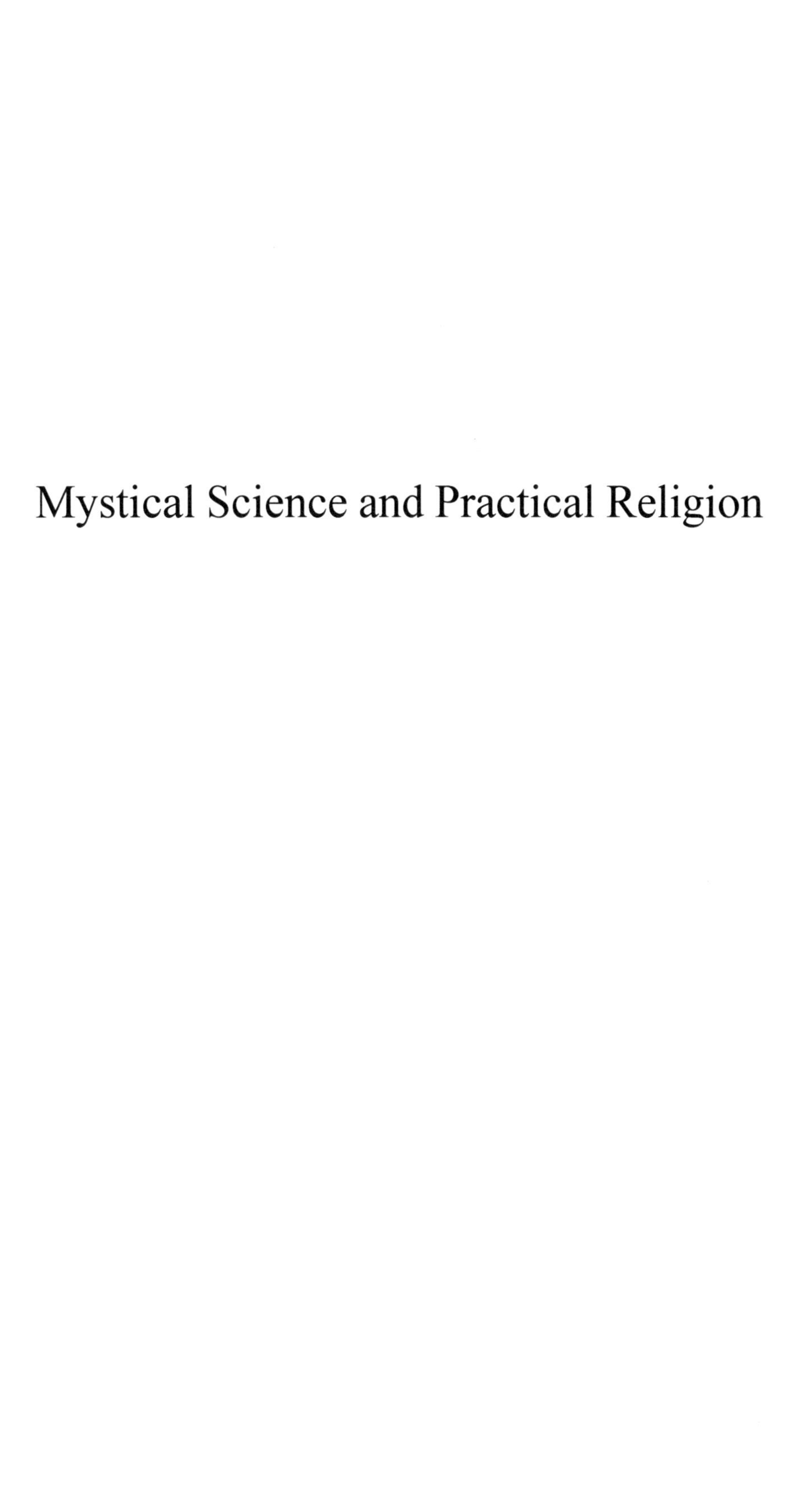

Mystical Science and Practical Religion

Mystical Science and Practical Religion

*Muslim, Hindu, and Sikh Discourse on
Science and Technology*

Richard Cimino

LEXINGTON BOOKS
Lanham • Boulder • New York • London

Published by Lexington Books
An imprint of The Rowman & Littlefield Publishing Group, Inc.
4501 Forbes Boulevard, Suite 200, Lanham, Maryland 20706
www.rowman.com

16 Carlisle Street, London W1D 3BT, United Kingdom

British Library Cataloguing in Publication Information Available

Library of Congress Cataloging-in-Publication Data

Cimino, Richard P.
Mystical science and practical religion : Muslim, Hindu, and Sikh discourse on science and technology / Richard Cimino.
p. cm.
Includes bibliographical references and index.
ISBN 978-0-7391-8227-7 (cloth : alk. paper)–ISBN 978-0-7391-8228-4 (ebook)
1. Religion and science. 2. Islam. 3. Hinduism. 4. Sikhism. 5. Technology–Religious aspects. I. Title.
BL240.3.C48 2014
201'.65–dc23
2014027539

Printed in the United States of America

Contents

Acknowledgments

This book has been a long time in coming, starting out as a dissertation and then being revised significantly, with various parts being published as articles and book chapters. In its early form as a dissertation in the Sociology department of the New School for Social Research, I would like to thank my advisor Jose Casanova for his encouragement and advice during the research and writing process. I am also grateful to Jeffrey Goldfarb for serving on my dissertation committee and for his generous assistance, particularly for the invitation to join his dissertation seminar. During my time at the New School, I also profited from the advice and feedback of numerous scholars, especially Fasil Devji, Anne Murphy, Sareeta Amrute, and Nilufer Gole.

Both before and after defending the dissertation in 2008, I presented this research at several conferences and seminars and significantly revised its chapters. An earlier and different version of chapter 2 was published in the book *Max Weber Matters* (ed. David Chalcraft et al., Ashgate, 2008). An earlier version of chapter 3 was published as a chapter in the *Religion and the Authority of Science* (ed. James Lewis, Brill, 2010). In writing these chapters and in the general revision of the manuscript, I would like to thank the many editors, anonymous reviewers, and friends who helped me hone and improve this work. In particular, my frequent collaborators and friends Christopher Smith and Daniel Varisco offered helpful criticisms of parts of the manuscript. At Lexington Books, I would like to thank Eric Wrona, Alissa Parra, Emily Frazzette, and Megan DeLancey for their advice, consideration, and patience.

As with my dissertation, I would like to dedicate this book to the memory of my cousin, Peter D'Agostino, who personified high scholarship and encouraged me (for better or worse!) to pursue the academic vocation. I am also grateful to my late parents, Stephen and Nancy, for always encouraging me to follow my interests and hoping for the best.

Introduction

Greeting me in the living room of his suburban Long Island home, Sarvjit, a recently retired civil engineer, summed up the thesis of my research a little too neatly before I even had told him much about it. "You'll see that I look at religion from the perspective of my profession and education," he said. "Everybody looks at religion from [the perspective of] their own professions . . . I'm an engineer, so things should add up. If it doesn't, then something is wrong."

I had spent over a year interviewing Muslim, Hindu, and Sikh engineers and Information Technology (IT) professionals, looking at the ways they related their work in technology and science to their religious lives. I doubted that the influence of occupation on religion proceeds in the strictly linear manner suggested by Sarvjit, but I was struck by his and others' self-assurance and matter-of-factness when discussing the relation between religion and science. I was also caught off guard by the fact that the Muslims, Hindus, and Sikhs I met tended to sound very much alike when they spoke about their faith and its relation to their work.

Few of them had much difficulty reconciling their work in technology and applied science with their particular religion, even claiming that science strengthened their personal faith. Theoretically, at least, this wasn't supposed to happen. Until fairly recently, it has been assumed that the advance of technology and science in general diminishes the vitality of religious belief and practice. As natural scientific explanations and actions (through technology) gained prominence and credence in modern societies, it was thought that the older supernatural explanations and their related rituals and practices would increasingly be seen as irrelevant artifacts. But this simple plotline has been complicated and confounded as the broader theory of secularization has been challenged. If religion is not in inevitable free fall under modernization, then the link between advancing science and secularity is also undone. And if that is the case, then the relation between science and religion becomes one of interaction rather than colonization and domination. It is not only a matter, as Sarvjit suggested, of scientific work shaping one's faith but also how scientific discourse is communicated and influenced by religious agency.

When I first started this project, I focused on the connection between fundamentalist Islam and Hinduism with work in applied science (for reasons which will be clear in the next two chapters). In my research and subsequent writing, I found a weak association between the two, at least in the United States. In fact, I have tried to throw doubt on the deterministic view that work in applied science points in a particular religious and ideological direction. By adding Sikhs to my research a year later, I wanted to include a greater representation of recent immigrant applied scientists. Adding Sikhism also provided greater room for comparison, which proved important in reaching some of my final conclusions.

As far as method was concerned, I also started out on a different track. I wanted not only to hear what the interviewees had to say about their work and their faith but also observe what they did—following them to their mosques and temples. While such participant-observation was attempted and carried out with the Hindu and Sikh cases, it was more difficult with the Muslims (let alone "fundamentalist" Muslims). It was very difficult getting Muslim contacts in the first place (possibly because of the fallout a few years after 9/11, when there was an inward turn among Musim communities), but it was also the case that several of the interviewees did not attend the same mosque on a regular basis (which is not required by the Islamic tradition) but rather worshipped in the closest mosque to where they were on particular Fridays.

But aside from these questions of method, I soon learned that dealing with how all of these professionals represented their beliefs and their work in the interviews (and in the related literature) was quite enough for my study. I was more convinced about the importance of their discourse and what it meant when I gradually began to see that the three religious-scientific discourses were very similar. They were linked by a high valuation of science shaped by the dynamics of immigration and integration into the American religious system and the professional class. At the same time, this discourse is marked by resistance to complete assimilation and the assertion of one's identity through claiming the scientific adaptability and even superiority of one's religion.

UNDERSTANDING RELIGIOUS-SCIENTIFIC DISCOURSE

Of course, when it comes to religion and science, we hear more about conflict than interaction, especially on such issues as evolution and biotechnology. My argument throughout this book is that understanding the context of the science-religion exchange is of great importance. For that reason, I look at one particular, though significant, corner of this encounter—the way in which these Muslim, Hindu, and Sikh professionals speak about their faith and work in applied science. But why specifically study applied science and these minority religions in the United States? Applied science is interesting for my purposes because it is based strongly on technology and rationality (in its efficiency and standardization) and is also an appealing field for religious believers. A growing share of applied science professionals in the American workforce and increasingly on the global level consists of immigrants and nationals from Asia, Southeast Asia, and the Middle East accompanied by their religious cultures of Islam, Hinduism, Sikhism, and Buddhism (and increasingly Christianity in the case of Asia). Thus, on a small scale, I want to examine the phenomenon of believers in global and often revitalized religions working in fields immersed in technology and "practical rationality."

I examine what can be called this "new knowledge class" of immigrants through in-depth interviews and content analysis of literature and websites produced by applied science professionals in the Muslim, Hindu, and Sikh communities. Since there has been scant research on this subject, the book provides both an exploratory study of these emerging professionals as well as, hopefully, a contribution to the fields of both immigration and "post-secularization," asking, in effect, if science and technology do not necessarily diminish religious vitality, then what do they do? The answer is complex, touching not only on matters of scientific work and religious identity, but also on the processes of immigration and globalization, and the particular "socio-logics" of Islam, Hinduism, Sikhism, and applied science itself.

But to simplify things before they get complicated, I have found that applied science, at least, is not as rational and practical, and also that religion is not as unscientific and impractical, as has been supposed. Both fields interact to create a more "religious" and ethical applied science and more "rational" and practical forms of Islam, Hinduism, and Sikhism. Although my investigation is on the level of discourse—how these science professionals speak about and represent their faith and work—it is also clear that they reproduce their ideas and values in their respective religious communities, particularly since embracing "science" is seen as a way of being both modern and religious in an American and a global context.

AN AFFINITY BETWEEN APPLIED SCIENCE AND RELIGION?

Whether as students, immigrant workers, or second-generation Americans, Muslim, Hindu, and Sikh engineers, doctors, and other applied scientists have emerged as a significant force in their religious communities. The entrance of these ethnic and religious groups into the fields of engineering, medicine, and computer science is not a uniquely American occurrence. Both sending and receiving nations are influential in channeling immigrant career trajectories, but the United States is an important destination for applied science students and those wishing to further their careers in the applied sciences. Since the Immigration Act of 1990, the United States experienced a sharp growth of professional immigrants, largely scientists, engineers, and health workers. In the United States as a whole, one-quarter of all computer programmers and engineers are foreign-born, according to Census figures. Indians and Chinese represent the highest percentage of such applied science professionals (Batalova and Lowell 2007).

In their home countries, applied science professionals, mainly engineers and IT professionals, have been active in religious and social movements. As we will see in the next two chapters, engineers and computer scientists have been prominent in the ranks of burgeoning religious revivalist or "fundamentalist" movements abroad. The transnational nature of immigration today brings these movements, as well as the broader traditions of Islam, Hinduism, and Sikhism themselves, into new forms of encounter with the West (Levitt 2007). But whether in the West or in Southeast Asia and the Middle East, applied science has proven to be especially amenable to religious believers.

The relationship between social strata (based on class, lifestyle and occupation) and religious orientation has been a persistent question in sociology since the pioneering work of Max Weber. He stated that knowledge is to a certain degree autonomous, and yet various social strata have often been the bearers of specific interests and ideas. The apparent contradiction between these two positions is resolved particularly in Weber's *Sociology of Religion*. It is in his writings on the historical shaping and patterning of the world religions where we find both concepts in play: those with certain economic and social interests may produce and convey specific kinds of religious knowledge. But while this knowledge may be related to certain interests and classes, the relation is not fixed; an "elective affinity" can develop between these ideas and other social strata (Weber 1978). This concept suggests that the forms of religious knowledge produced by applied scientists may have a wider application, especially given these professionals' prominence in their communities.

This study investigates the nature and extent of the relationship between religion and science as it is fleshed out in the work and lives of applied science practitioners. Theories in the sociology of knowledge have posited scientific practices and knowledge as being socially bounded and as serving a legitimizing function for institutions and the wider social order. Thus, my research seeks to show how scientific knowledge can be influenced by religious beliefs as well as how scientific concepts and professional status can be used to shape religious discourse and teachings. In a broader context, I am interested in how these interactions between applied science and religion may help explain how such faiths as Islam, Hinduism, and Sikhism are being recast as they take root in the West.

THREE MODELS OF RELIGION-SCIENCE INTERACTION

The question of whether technology and science inherently conflicts with religion is addressed in most of the literature of secularization. There are three main theories or models that have been developed concerning the relationship of religion and applied science. Such classical sociologists as Durkheim and Weber tended to see at least the cognitive elements of religion becoming marginalized by the forces of rationalization and differentiation of modernity, even though they did not see science as replacing religion (Weber 1978; Durkheim 1965). In the modern era, Peter Berger, when he was still a proponent of the secularization theory, saw the technological worldview as complementing the secular mentality under modernization and, more important, pluralization. Berger, Berger, and Kellner (1973) argued that the cognitive dimensions of technology threaten religious beliefs and a sense of the sacred. The segregation of work-related functions from other parts of one's life and the anonymity of being a cog in the wheel of the production process all work to create a sense of meaningless and anomie that are opposed to the religious consciousness. While they question whether there is an intrinsic and inevitable opposition between religion and technology and science, the forces unleashed by modernization challenge the "mystery, magic and authority . . . important for religiosity." Thus, the plausibility of religious definitions of reality is threatened not only by the "pluralization of lifeworlds," but also by the rationalization that is integral to modernity.

Bryan Wilson has cited Weber's concepts to suggest that secularization is strongly associated with the rise of the natural sciences and its technical specification, standardization, and routinization of procedures with the aim of replicating outcomes. Such rationalization is present even when science is put to religious ends, such as in blending religion with the psychotherapeutic concepts of self-improvement. By catering to "this worldly" needs—be it well-being or economic success—religion is yielding to instrumental and utilitarian thinking (Wilson 1982).

But more recently, secularization theorists have placed much less emphasis on the role of science and rationalization in general in this process. Bruce (2002) mainly correlates religious and cultural pluralism with secularization. Norris and Inglehart (2004) hardly mention science as a causal factor in secularization, and, in fact, find a higher estimation of the role of scientific advancement among highly religious (particularly Islamic) societies than in secular northern European countries. More recently, Berger (2012) has modified his theory on pluralization to argue that a "default secular discourse coexists with a plurality of religious discourses," which suggests that modern people, including scientists, "alternate between secular and religious definitions of reality." Thus, Berger would see a practicing Muslim scientist's weekly pilgrimage from the laboratory to the mosque as being little different than the transitions most people make between religious and secular thinking and discourse.

Recent studies on the religious beliefs and practices of scientists also add more complexity to the science-religion relationship. Ecklund (2010) found that those viewing science and religion in a conflict model represented only a minority of such professionals; the younger generations of scientists were actually less likely to hold to an antagonistic relationship between the two fields. Smith (2003) and Evans and Evans (2008) argue that the conflict between religion and science can be best understood as taking place between institutions with conflicting interests and agendas. In this perspective, the degree to which science or religion wins the most confidence of the public is determined more by the competition between scientific and religious institutions and their respective strategies to gain resources and legitimacy than by the inherent validity of their concepts.

The second theory that has been developed has generated less literature, but it is increasingly prominent in studies of fundamentalism (as we will see in chapter 1). This theory holds that applied science, because of its value-neutral and instrumental nature, has a special affinity for conservative and fundamentalist believers who seek to avoid the challenges of more humanistic fields (i.e., psychology and sociology) as well as the natural sciences which may challenge their beliefs, whether on the origins of the earth or the divine source of morality. Implied in the separation of applied science from these other fields is that the former is based on a form of rationality that is largely utilitarian. Applied science, like capitalism, is thought to operate outside the realm of values and meaning, focusing on questions of efficiency, precision and instrumental outcomes (i.e., does it work?). Of course, science in general is viewed in these terms by classical sociology. The disenchantment caused by the advancement of science's theoretical rationalism and its ever-growing explanations of reality is similar to economic rationalism's "iron cage" in Weber's *The Protestant Ethic and the Spirit of Capitalism*. It could be argued that applied science, which is wed more closely to capitalism in its development, takes even a more utilitarian approach than theoretical science. In this field it is particularly easy to compartmentalize one's religious beliefs and worldviews apart from one's work in the practical sciences of engineering and computer science.

The final theory or model tends to see religion and science (including applied science) in a complementary relationship. These theorists have argued that the history, development, and construction of the various disciplines of modern science—including applied science—account for much of the conflict as well as affinities between religion and science. In his study on Puritanism, pietism, and science, Robert Merton (1962) argues that the empirical and rational approach of these streams of Protestantism lent themselves to the newly emerging technological and scientific outlook. Merton views the impact of Protestants upon the emerging scientific outlook in a similar way to that of Max Weber's study of early Calvinists and other sects' role in shaping the ethic of capitalism. He notes that, like Weber's Protestant ethic, there is not a straight line between Puritanism and science. Luther, Calvin and other early Protestant leaders did not support many of the scientific discoveries of their times. Calvin's theocratic Geneva and the strongly conservative forms of Calvinism that later emerged (among the Baptists, for instance), in fact, may have impeded the development of science. Yet a scientific ethic emerged as these Puritan and pietist values encouraged the utilitarian motives of empiricism and rationalism (Merton 1962). But even if the utilitarian motivations competed with and overtook Christian values and language, the basic point of Merton's research is that conflict is not the only relation between science and religion. The science of Elizabethan England could develop "within the bounds set by the religious doctrine of the time."

Most of the empirical research on science practitioners and religion has focused on academic scientists. Since only a small segment of applied scientists are in academic fields (engineering, computer science and medical school professors and students), this quantitative research may not be representative of all applied science professionals. Nevertheless, survey research does show the differences among the various disciplines on questions of religious belief and practice, with engineering professors rating higher than most other disciplines in religiosity (Zinsmeister 2005; Wuthnow 1985; Vaughan, Smith, and Sjoberg 1966). More recently, professors in the academic fields of nursing, finance, and accounting show more religiosity, although engineering still ranks higher than other science disciplines (Gross and Simmons 2009; Gross 2013). Such results suggest the institutional nature of secularization. This embedded nature of secularization can be understood historically, as institutional actors by their own agency shape policies and make decisions that move certain professions and spheres of society in more secular or religious directions (Smith 2003).

Wuthnow (1985) has found that the shift to religious nonconventionality and non-belief takes place not as part of the socialization process into those academic science careers but prior to it. In a survey of students in Berkeley, California, Wuthnow found that those majoring in the social sciences were most likely to have been raised in nonreligious families; humanities students were most likely to have defected from the religion in which they were brought up, and natural science students were more likely to have retained their religious faith. Other research on the political and religious attitudes of applied scientists suggests continued difference from other academics. For this reason, Wuthnow's theory of boundary maintenance, though questionable as an overall explanation, may be helpful in understanding the religious differences across disciplines and professions.

According to Wuthnow, all scientists have to engage in "reality maintenance" and legitimation of their disciplines in the face of "everyday reality." One mechanism of reality-maintenance is the codification of a theoretical paradigm which lays down certain research problems, promotes communication, and clarifies standards of evaluation and reward. Codification is high in the natural sciences and lower in the social sciences and humanities. For this reason, social scientists rely more on values, attitudes and lifestyles to "maintain the reality of science by setting up external boundaries between themselves and the general public or those who represent the realm of everyday reality," Wuthnow writes. Such an attitude as irreligiosity helps to "maintain the plausibility of the scientific province by differentiating scientists (in their own minds) from the larger public who represent everyday reality and generally maintain stronger religious identifications" (Wuthnow 1985: 196–197).

While there is some debate on the validity of boundary maintenance theory, past research suggests how it might help explain the higher rate of religiosity among applied scientists. A study of Texan Petroleum engineers (Constant 1989) found that they were largely drawn from the ranks of the sons of oil workers. Even after their university educations, these engineers shared in the values and lifestyles of the surrounding oil culture in which they worked, including a preference for "fundamentalist" Christian denominations. The pattern of affiliation with Baptist and Methodist churches was higher among the engineering graduates from the University of Texas than that of the student body in general. Thus, these engineers truly represented "science in society"—on one hand, working with a body of highly codified, sophisticated, "differentiated and stratified knowledge," while, on the other hand, "sharing remarkable localite and homogenous cultural origins." Wilensky and Ladinsky (1967) posit that engineering is weak in professionalism—as compared with lawyers and professors—and strong in careerism. Thus, the work of engineers has little to do with the "transmission or mediation of core values" and they do not share the sense of a "calling" as a professor or lawyer might, which can serve as a secular substitute for religion. From these few examples, one can see how sociologists have been hard pressed in categorizing engineering as a profession or career, not to mention capturing its liminal nature existing between science, industry, craft, and management (most engineers move to management levels in the second half of their careers). Things are complicated further when considering computer science; some programmers, especially those working for small software firms, can be considered entrepreneurs, while lower status computer technicians have been called the new working class (Keefe and Potosky 1997; Thornton 1999). All of these complexities make it difficult to draw a straight line between profession and religious outcomes.

As we will see in the next chapter, recent scholarly and popular treatments of fundamentalism also assert the complementary nature of this kind of religion with applied science. Without much explanation of causal factors behind this relationship, the link between fundamentalist Christianity and applied science was made in a study on the social base of support for a New Christian Right group in Oregon by Burris (2001). The study found engineers to be the most over-represented professional category (3.5 times the proportion in the state), with the largest share of these professionals being engineers in the computer and electronic firms around the city of Portland. In citing a history of the evangelical campus ministry, InterVarsity in Britain, noting that most of its early patrons were doctors or engineers, Steve Bruce argues that the cognitive style of conservative Protestantism, with its stress on an orderly universe (and biblical text) that yields knowable facts, converges with the inductive method of the applied sciences, which he characterizes as a "mundane science" as opposed to the "advanced science" of biology and physics. In the same text, Bruce makes the connection between fundamentalist Islam and applied science (Bruce 2002).

STUDYING TECHNOSCIENCE PROFESSIONALS AND THEIR RELIGIONS

Some of the above conclusions about the relations between applied science and religion are largely drawn from commonsense assumptions and anecdotal accounts and lack an empirical foundation. Such observations also tend to collapse the various applied science professions together or link them with non–applied science fields (architecture or business). Some of these analyses cast doubt on the "true" scientific nature of the applied sciences or underline the materialistic and deterministic nature of these professionals' faith (i.e., being a form of secular therapy). But it does not seem to be the place for a sociological investigation to question the validity of either the science of the religionists or the religion of the applied scientists. Following in the tradition of W. I. Thomas, I would agree that if people "define situations as real, they are real in their consequences (quoted in Merton 1995: 380)." Peter Van der Veer (2005: 289) is writing in regard to Hinduism and science but his words also apply to the other religions under study in this book: "There is no reason at all to expect Hindu engineers and scientists to 'lose their religion' and become secular. Hindu modernity includes an ideological valuation of science and technology. The empirical question is rather to explore what religion does for them; what kind of specific needs it produces or addresses."

Since I was primarily interested in the religious discourse of Muslim, Hindu and Sikh applied science professionals, my preferred method was formal interviews. I also conducted textual analyses of their writings, particularly as they are found on the Internet. I conducted forty-five interviews with Muslim, Hindu and Sikh engineers and Information Technology (IT) professionals, professors and students. I interviewed five graduate students and one undergraduate student (two studying engineering and four studying computer science), six professors (three in computer science, two in mechanical engineering, and one in applied mathematics), one academic researcher (in computer linguistics) and thirty-three professionals (three of whom were also attending school part-time in business and computer science). Among the professionals, twelve worked in engineering, twenty worked in IT, though it should be noted that several of the IT professionals had educations and early careers in engineering. Four of the professionals were recently retired.

Almost all of the subjects were immigrants who arrived in the United States between 1968 and 2004. Only two of the Sikh interviewees were born in the United States. The home countries of the foreign-born subjects are: India for all the Sikh and Hindu interviewees, and Egypt (three), Pakistan (five), India (two), Saudi Arabia (one), Jordan (one), Iran (one), Turkey (two) for the Muslims. Four of the interviewees were women. All of the interviewees were self-professing and practicing Muslims, Hindus, and Sikhs. I define "practicing Muslims, Hindus, and Sikhs" by the subjects' own self-definitions and identification with their religious communities, as well as adherence to basic teachings and practices. For the Muslims, all of the interviewees made an attempt to engage in the basic practices of Islam—fasting, prayer, study of the Koran (I also cite a non-practicing Muslim I interviewed who is not included in the sample of fifteen subjects). Not all of the self-professing Hindus were active in their communities, but they cited religious reasons (i.e., wrong interpretations of the Vedas) for their non-involvement. All of the Sikhs were involved in their religious communities (i.e., at least occasionally attending gudwaras or other Sikh gatherings), and held to the authority of the Sikh sacred text, the Guru Granth.

The interviews were conducted mainly in the offices of these professionals or in neutral meeting places (i.e., university cafeterias, diners, and coffee shops), and occasionally in their places of worship or their homes. The interviews lasted approximately one hour (ranging from thirty minutes to three hours) and took place in the New York metropolitan area (including New Jersey) from October 2005 to December 2007. All of the interviewees agreed to the interviews beforehand and to the following conditions: that their responses would be used in my initial dissertation and in subsequent published writings, and that pseudonyms would be used for their real names.

A good part of the sample for the interviews was obtained through the snowball method, as subjects referred me to other potential interviewees. I also located about one-quarter of the interviewees through contacting engineering and computer science departments at universities in the New York area. The interviews, which were recorded by hand, were open-ended and based around these professionals' and students' self-understandings of their religious beliefs and practices. I was as interested in how they apply their faith to their work as in how their work and professional lives (including their educations) shaped their religious discourse.

For instance, how did they interpret sacred texts and what elements of their religious lives did they emphasize and de-emphasize (prayer, meditation, and scripture reading)? It was particularly important to take note of the conceptual language used to describe their faith, and whether there was much of a crossover between their scientific language and concepts and their religious discourse. Did they see any conflicts between their work and their faith? If so, how do they deal with these conflicts? How did they view the relationship between science, technology, and religion in general? It was also especially crucial to find out how the interviewees related to the authorities of their respective religious communities: In other words, what sources did they turn to when they had questions and dilemmas about their faith?

I also attempted to conduct participant-observation of larger gatherings and services that are pertinent to my subject. This is especially the case for the Hindu and Sikh chapters, since several of my interviews were conducted in or near temples. Along with the discourses from the interviews, I also examined literature written by these and other applied science professionals, including material featured on the Internet. These included popular websites such as *Sikh.net, Islam Online, Hindu.org,* and print publications, such as *Hinduism Today.* I sought out this material to ascertain whether the interviewees' discourses and views were widely shared outside of my sample. While the interviews and content analysis may not be representative of all Muslim, Hindu, and Sikh applied scientists, I believe they richly illuminate the discourse employed by these professionals in discussing their faith and its intersection with their work. Finally, an attempt was made to support my findings with other ethnographic and survey research. As indicated earlier, there have been only a few studies that focus on applied science and religion in the United States, but it was possible to find other studies that either examine significant aspects of my subject (for instance, Muslim attitudes in the United States) or look at similar groups of professionals in other countries.

HOW THIS BOOK IS ORGANIZED

The first three chapters of this book introduce the case studies of the Muslim, Hindu, and Sikh professionals I interviewed. Each chapter integrates discussions and analyses surrounding the accounts of my interviews. Since neither religion nor science is generic, whether standing alone or in their interactions with each other, the chapters engage particular aspects of the science-religion relationship as they pertain to these various faith traditions.

In chapter 1 on the Muslims, I pay particular attention to the claim that Islamic fundamentalism has an affinity with applied science. In contrast, I find, at least in the case of American Muslims, that religious pragmatism rather than fundamentalism or extremism is more likely to typify involvement in such work.

In chapter 2, I examine how mystical and ritual-based Hinduism adapts to the standards of practical rationality as its practitioners enter the worlds of IT and engineering. Such an encounter changes both the discourse of traditional Hinduism and that of applied science. In the last section of this chapter, I also look at the relation between Hindu nationalism or fundamentalism and these applied science professionals.

As a religion positioned between Islam and Hinduism, Sikhism, the subject of chapter 3, has tended to differentiate itself from both faiths. We see this in the Sikh professionals' stress on communal identity and social justice over spirituality. Meanwhile, the Sikhs' entrepreneurial ethic has led them to management and ownership levels of engineering and IT firms, making Max Weber's classic questions about the dilemmas of the religious creation of wealth and prosperity particularly pertinent.

In chapter 4, I compare and contrast the Muslim, Hindu and Sikh cases, discussing the complex interactions deriving from immigration, transnationalism, and globalization that play a part in shaping their discourse. While I find a common religion-science discourse employed by these professionals, I also pay attention to the way each faith (rather than "religion" in general) has a particular logic and repertoire from which the professional draws as they face the challenges of their work. At the same time, the professionals are influenced by broader forces that are reshaping their faiths, such as "de-traditionalization." I end this chapter by arguing that applied science itself is not as rational as supposed but rather a set of practices and principles that vary according to context—including religious contexts.

The conclusion offers a summary of my findings and a closing argument about the future of religion and applied science in a global context, looking specifically at the role of these religious applied scientists in their respective communities, taking evangelical Christianity as an example of this process.

Chapter One

American Muslim Applied Science Professionals and the Spirit of Pragmatism

Recent sociological inquiry into the relationship between science and religion has focused on the theme of conflict, often involving the natural and social sciences (Ecklund 2010, Evans 2008). In other fields, especially applied science, the interactions between religion and science are less conflict-ridden, if no less complex. As I discuss in the introduction, applied science has traditionally attracted far more believers to its ranks than its theoretical siblings. In fact, applied science has been associated with conservative and even "fundamentalist" religion (Bruce 2002; Burris 2001; Constant 1989). This is especially the case with Islam, where sociologists have argued that there is a link between work in engineering and IT with extremist expressions of the religion (Gambetta and Hertog 2009; Sivan 1985).

In this chapter, I address the emerging debates and research on the place of Islam in science and use applied science as a case study in how these two fields interact beyond the expected directions of secularization or fundamentalism. I attempt to show how the way in which applied science professionals speak about their faith and work, especially in an American context, calls into question past and current assumptions about the role of technology in shaping or challenging religious beliefs. I argue that three basic theories that have been used to explain the relation between science and religion—that of conflict, neutrality, and compatibility—do not capture the complexity in this relationship. My analysis of the discourse of Muslim applied scientists suggests that such professionals tend to take a more pragmatic rather than ideological approach to their faith, one that is influenced by a range of occupational, immigration, and religious factors. This does not mean that conflicts between Islam and modern science are not evident in this discourse. Yet the values of practicality and empiricism that form the "institutional logic" of this field, as well its linkage with aspirations of upward educational and occupational mobility among immigrants, influence the religious discourse of these Muslim professionals, moving them away from religious extremism. While my focus is on religious discourse and not on organizational behavior, I employ the concept of institutional logic to suggest that "institutions, through their underlying logics of action, shape heterogenieity, stability, and change in individuals and organizations" (Thornton and Ocasio 2008: 103). In my examination of these Muslim professionals' discourse on the relation between their faith and work, I will seek to show how the seemingly competing institutional logics of religion and applied science are reconciled on a cognitive and subjective level.

HARD SCIENCE AND STRONG RELIGION

Islam has had a long and complex relationship with science. While there is not a Koranic or Islamic science in the same way that there is a "Vedic science" in Hinduism, Islam, as elucidated in the Koran and the Sunnah (sayings of Mohommad), was seen as embracing a comprehensive knowledge about the world (Cook 2014). The rational and empirical approach of the Koran has been seen as formative in inspiring scientific discoveries and insights, particularly in the Islamic "golden age" from the eighth to the sixteenth centuries. Olivier Roy (1994) suggests that more recently, the Muslim entrance onto scientific career paths, particularly engineering and information technology, has been precarious, with less transnational networking and connections taking place as compared to other immigrants from South and East Asia. The higher educational structures in which Muslims in the Middle East and South Asia are trained are usually state-sponsored and are established along Western lines. But science education in general in Muslim countries has lagged behind the West due to a host of economic, political, and social factors. Whereas Western societies were able to integrate the lower middle classes graduating from the mass educational system into a "differentiated 'trade' or 'professional' status," the high expectations of Muslim students have been largely frustrated. The lack of industry, administrative positions, or even more traditional vocations (due, for instance, to a devaluation of religious schooling) in these societies often means that education "bestows neither knowledge nor power nor status," writes Roy. In such situations, emigration, either to graduate school or to work in the West, becomes attractive, as do other options—either becoming involved in "political contestation, or, as a last resort, withdrawal to [an Islamic] sect" (Roy 1994: 94).

Yet most literature would see the relationship between Muslims and applied science and technology as involving instrumental and utilitarian purposes. The Fundamentalism Project, a series of studies and books on the phenomenon of fundamentalism around the world, portrayed Muslim involvement in technology and science as either one of instrumental use and neutrality or attempting to forge a particularly Islamic science (Tibi 1993; Rajaee 1993). Riesebrodt (1993) compared Protestant fundamentalism in the United States with Shi'ite Islamic fundamentalism in Iran and concluded that both see technology as ethically neutral and not necessarily a depersonalizing or force detrimental to their faith.

In studies of the emergence of radical Islamic groups in the Middle East in the 1970s and 1980s, the presence of science and engineering students stands out. In a study of Sayyid Qutb's Muslim Brotherhood in Egypt, two-thirds had education in the sciences and engineering. Of 326 members of the Jihad Organization of Egypt, 62 percent had a higher education and 55 percent of the university students were in the more modern disciplines of science, engineering, and medicine. The more moderate and liberal Muslims were often students of literature and other liberal arts (Sivan 1985). The most recent and extensive research by Gambetta and Hertog (2009) confirms the disproportionate involvement of engineers in Islamist groups up to the present day. Through compiling information on the educational attainment of 178 members and participants in violent non-Western Islamist groups, they found that engineering was the most popular field of study (78 out of the 178 studied engineering, compared with fourteen cases in medicine, twelve in economics and business, and seven in natural sciences). Although Western-based Muslim extremists had low educational levels, engineering also showed up as the predominant profession.

These "new radicals" were comfortable in the modern world, yet they refused to accept modernist Islam that supported interaction and compromise with the West. Even traditionalist Muslims accepted technology in principle, if not the values deriving from it, but the engineering and science backgrounds of the radicals pushed them further in feeling "no unease or qualms about using modern technologies that could be turned against the rulers, from the use of audio media, to the smuggling and dissemination of ideas (in what is still essentially an oral culture), to terrorism." In contrast, the modernist Muslims were from literary backgrounds and their ignorance of technology was no match for the radicals (Sivan 1985).

The most recent theory concerning Islam and applied science is that the two fields complement each other. Gambetta and Hertog (2009) go so far as to find a universal "engineering mindset," which predisposes such professionals to political conservatism and religiosity, as well as a penchant for "orderly patterns" and simple solutions—the same characteristics that mark much of Islamic fundamentalism and radicalism. Gambetta and Hertog also cite the frustration and "relative deprivation" of engineers in Islamic societies that make little room for such a profession as an accompanying factor in such radicalism (Saudi Arabia, which provides demand and support for engineers, showed a low correlation between engineering and Islamism). Edis (2007) similarly critiques the high valuation of technology and science among Muslims as a way of making themselves modern even while they hold "pseudoscientific" views on such matters as evolution and miracles.

While not questioning the scientific nature of the applied science profession, Eickelman and Anderson (1999) argue that the new professionals in Islam in the United States present "Islamic doctrines and discourse in accessible, vernacular terms." Thus, Islamic discourse has "become reframed in styles of reasoning and forms of argument that draw on wider, less exclusive or erudite bodies of knowledge."

Studies of the leadership in mosques have documented the rise of a new professional class of Muslims that has ideological ramifications for Islam in America. The emergence of Muslim applied science professionals as a social force in the American Islamic community has mainly been driven by South Asian immigration. The South Asians were more highly educated than the earlier Arab Muslims and they also stood out as the most conservative of Muslims. According to Leonard (2003), these more recent Muslim immigrants created a shift or "interruption" in a pattern of Muslim "assimilation" or accommodation to American society. This trend toward more observant and conservative Islam can be at odds with traditional modes of leadership and transmission of the faith. A traditional emphasis on the imams (leaders) in mosques showing a high standard of theological learning has now given way to leadership positions (such as found on the board of directors in mosques) occupied by engineers, medical doctors, and other professionals. Studies of Islam on the Internet by Bunt (2003), Anderson (2005), and Varisco (2010), find that Muslim computer scientists, who were early innovators of this technology, tend to control the discourse on Islamic websites and online forums. They apply techniques acquired in their technical education to interpreting texts, without the traditional "textual hermeneutics of madrasa training" (Anderson 2005). The proficiency of Muslim applied scientists on the Internet has given them greater exposure to a global Islamic community where revivalist and sometimes extremist tendencies are pronounced, especially in the early stage of this communications technology (Lofti 2002). In comparing the rhetoric of Islamic preachers on the website of the missionary movement Tavlighi Jama'at of Pakistan, P. D. Gaffney (1994) found a "warrior style" distinct from both scholarly and spiritual styles by its this-worldly focus drawing on practical knowledge and based largely on scientific and medical allusion. There is also a good deal of anecdotal information on the influence of the "new professionals" in mosques and other organizations. From a political science perspective, Khan (2002) portrays such an organization as the Islamic Circle of North America, where the South Asian influence is the most evident, as "forming a normative elite" in American Islam. Other literature reports on a growing negative reaction among Muslims regarding the new professional elite. Some Muslims have been disturbed that young people are being steered toward the professions of medicine and engineering and away from other fields (Athar 1997). The professional leadership of American Muslim organizations and mosques is sometimes criticized as having medical, business, or computer technology training rather than knowledge and Wisdom" (Leonard 2003: 20).

ISLAM, SCIENCE, AND PRAGMATISM

My research suggests that the three theories on the relation of religion and applied science, as discussed in the introduction, lack the complexity to deal with the discourse and beliefs of Muslim professionals in the United States I propose a more interactive model that takes into account both the particular contexts of Islam and applied science as they are practiced and have developed in the United States.

This does not mean that these theories cannot shed some light on the religious discourse and practices of these professionals. The interviewees' accounts of taking up the applied sciences as a way of avoidance and even protection from "ungodly" and secularist perspectives in other disciplines and professions was most strongly voiced by one undergraduate and two Muslim graduate students who were still weighing their career choices and also tended to be the most conservative of my sample (for instance, in dress and support of ideological conservatism, if not Islamism); such views were less emphasized (although not absent) among the rest of the professionals already established in these fields.

Nazir, a twenty-five-year-old graduate student in computer science at a state university, grew up in a devout, middle-class Muslim home in Jordan. His father was a businessman and a pious believer, and Nazir continued such devotion in his own life. When he came to the United States in 2004 to attend college, Nazir first felt cut off from his family and faith. It was his involvement in the Muslim Student Association (MSA) on campus that has both sustained his faith and provided a social network. "I felt like less of a stranger," Nazir said. Today, all his friends in school are fellow Muslims. He has become a leader of the MSA, sometimes leading the Friday prayer services. He now has a long beard—in honor of Mohammad—and when I met him he was wearing loose-fitting white clothes and a prayer cap—attire that more traditional Muslim men wear.

Nazir values Islam because of its call for people to submit to God. "You have to take it as a whole. . . . [You] can't choose one part [of the faith]." Yet he does not feel that his community of faith judges him when he cannot measure up to its standards. "Like with fasting, nobody is going to judge you if you don't do it. But [the practice] shows discipline." In explaining the connection between his chosen field of study and his faith, Nazir said: "One good thing about what I'm doing is that we have no contradictions [between Islam and computer science]. It's a non-controversial field; it's practical." Following the teachings of his imam, Nazir said there are two kinds of knowledge: "practical knowledge" and "philosophical knowledge." It is the latter that one "has to be careful about. The problem with philosophical knowledge is that you have to be careful when scientists go beyond their limit—like evolution. . . . The good thing about the computer science field is that it's all about facts and tools for doing things."

The uneasiness with other disciplines and the challenge they may pose to Islam extended to the natural sciences. In this case, however, the applied science was not just a neutral field for religious believers but actually functioned to bolster their faith. Without much knowledge of Middle Eastern names and having only arranged our interview by email, I was surprised when a student by the name of Aysel introduced herself to me at the train station near her Ivy League university. Aside from being female in a largely male-dominated field of study, the twenty-nine-year-old chemical engineering doctoral student straddled the secular-religious boundary in other ways. Aysel, who came to study in the United States from Turkey and whose father was an engineer, admitted that she was neither involved with the more conservative Muslim community on campus nor with non-Muslim students or groups and did not wear a head covering. She maintained a solitary practice of Islam, seeing the faith as a source of strength and hope during periods of depression even as she felt her grasp of it was weak and unstable; she said she was "not courageous enough" to wear a head covering on campus. Aysel had a fairly liberal upbringing until her teenage years, when her family became observant Muslims, reflecting the Islamic revival that Turkey has experienced in recent years. During a brief and unhappy marriage she stopped practicing the faith. But gradually she returned to a more observant life framed around study of the Koran, fasting, and prayer five times a day.

Aysel viewed the natural sciences, such as biology, as "materialistic" and fields such as computer science and engineering as less "risky" to her faith. But she also emphasized the positive nature of engineering in relation to her faith. Rather than just providing an escape from contested issues of faith, reason, and science, Aysel saw her field of study as validating Islam: "Everything I do reminds me of how hard it is to predict things and [shows] me God's beauty and power. It's not only in my work but just in [watching] a spider. What we're trying to do is mimic these things. A big part of engineering is mimicking; we look at all these things around us and how they work. I deal with the real laws God [made] to govern things, so I'm seeing God's design in things."

INCOMPLETE AND PROVISIONAL SCIENCE

Aysel's story suggests that it is not only a matter of work in applied science and technology shielding these believers from intellectual and cognitive challenges to the faith. Rather, there is an interaction between these two fields, with these professionals often affirming and developing as much as compartmentalizing in the workplace and classroom. In other words, they could frame their insights in both the secular language of applied science as well as in the spiritual language of the believer when speaking to fellow Muslims or to this interviewer. It is the case that almost all of the Muslim applied science professionals and students I spoke with compared the flexible and "faith-friendly" nature of engineering and computer science with the more critical approach of the natural sciences toward religion. In fact, both their practical scientific orientation and their religious beliefs significantly shaped the way they viewed science in general. This is most evident in their discussion of evolution.

"I've never met a Muslim who believed in evolution," said Tariq in a matter-of-fact tone toward the end of our interview in his office at a Long Island business college. Like most of the other interviewees, Tariq grew up in a practicing Muslim home in Egypt. Although he was a professor of computer science and information systems, he was certain that "science will come around to the truth [of creationism]; it's all so clear-cut." Edis (2007) argues that creationism and intelligent design are more widely accepted in education, the media, and intellectual circles in Muslim nations than among Christians in the United States, although the high rates of Americans opposing evolution regularly on display in opinion polls suggests a stubborn resistance to the theory. Such Muslim creationist apologists as Adnan Oktar of Turkey have packaged creation science as a sophisticated scientific answer to evolution for technologically savvy and modern Muslims around the world. Both in Christianity and Islam, engineers and other applied scientists, including doctors, have had a distinctive role in challenging and proposing alternatives to evolution, most notably through the creationist and intelligent design movements (Edis 2007; Akyol 2004; Shanavas 2005; Witham 2002). For instance, a 2005 study of 1,482 American medical doctors found that 34 percent agreed more with intelligent design than Darwinian evolution. For the Muslim physicians in this sample, this number rose to 73 percent (though there was a sample of only forty Muslim doctors in the survey) (Edis 2007).

Yet if one is on the Internet for any length of time, it is not difficult to "meet" many Muslims who hold a variety of views on the origins of the earth and humanity. A recent study of Pakistani-American physicians found that most accepted evolution but they also applied various meanings to the theory, including the view that Allah created the world through the evolutionary process (Everhart and Hameed 2013). Even among the interviewees, I found responses ranging from strict creationism to intelligent design, which held a special attraction to engineers, to theistic evolution. Yet evolution is a theory that many Muslims as well as Christians have had problems accepting. Evolution was viewed by interviewees as the issue that caused the most personal conflicts relating to science and religion, even though most did not work in areas affected by this debate. Fatima, an Egyptian-born computational linguist at an Ivy League university, recalls that when she took a linguistics course in graduate school, the subject turned to inborn language traits among infants. When the professor asked the class about what other theories could explain such language skills, Fatima volunteered that perhaps the trait was a product of creation rather than evolution. "I just saw mouths drop [in the class]. But I thought as scientists we should look at all possibilities." Fatima did not hold a strictly literalist creationist view. She was most congenial to the idea of intelligent design, though adding an Islamic caveat. "God didn't just create and then go away. In Islam He is the sustainer, always intervening and involved; that's the extra punch of Islam."

Ahmed, a forty-three-year-old electrical engineer originally from India who worked at a New Jersey telecommunications firm, argued that since one of the attributes of Allah as "sustainer" can also be translated as "evolver," he has no problem with most aspects of evolution. Yet the theory of evolution and creation he worked out combined random and local variation in nature with a good deal more "intelligent design" and structure when it came to the creation of humans. Aysel, the chemical engineering doctoral student, said she "totally rejects the idea of people developing from lower forms of life," while Shafiq, a fifty-two-year-old civil engineer from Pakistan, found more room and flexibility in the Koran to allow for the possibility. "It's not clear. The Koran teaches that Adam was in a lifeless state. So there are hints that there was something before human beings, but it doesn't venture to say what. I don't see any conflict with evolution. The theme [of evolution] isn't specified in the Koran, so it doesn't close the door on it."

The interviewees made the frequent claim that modern science and its approach to evolution has too easily made the unwarranted jump from scientific evidence to philosophical attacks against religion. These applied scientists also tended to see science as more open-ended and unstable, believing that even a central theory such as evolution was far from settled and could be reversed.

Thus, Nazir, the computer science student, said the "scientific proof is not strong enough yet" for evolution. He also was sure that "eventually, evolution is going to be refuted. The first people thought the earth was flat. The

Koran found that the earth was more like an egg. But in a thousand years, people did realize the earth is oval shaped." The view that the Koran foreshadowed scientific truths that were later validated by modern science was common among most of these interviewees. In a study of religion and science in the Muslim world, Turkish physicist Edis (2007) notes that "Muslim apologists" who argue that scientific discoveries are foreshadowed in the scriptures are popular among Muslims throughout the world, perhaps more so than among Christians and other religions because of the strongly text-based nature of Islam. But what stood out more during the interviews was how these professionals claim they are actually being more open-minded and scientific than the established science community by making room for "unorthodox" and speculative views. This tendency is related to the applied science focus on practical knowledge often to the exclusion of theoretical knowledge. In this context, it is not a huge leap for the engineer or programmer who is also a believer to see intentional design rather than random selection and chance as the principle way things come into existence.

As with other respondents, Salman, a twenty-eight-year-old computer science student from India, said that "science helps reinforce religious belief." He also shared a view common among interviewees about the way in which work in designing software, machines, chemicals and materials gave them a greater appreciation for the complexity of things and the belief in God as the ultimate designer. They shared the view that there are laws and an underlying design in nature and creation that can be uncovered and then, to a certain degree, mimicked and reproduced. Yet Salman was critical of attempts to view the Koran as a book of science. "It's a book of moral guidance. The risk in seeing science in the Koran is that science is shameless in the [way that] it changes. If you say the Koran predicted [something], the problem is that you mutilate verses to make it true. The Koran doesn't need validation by saying it's confirming science."

ISLAMIC SCIENCE OR SCIENTIFIC ISLAM?

In recent years, there has been much written on the "Islamicization of knowledge." Stenberg (1996) writes that both in the United States and in Islamic societies, Muslim theologians and philosophers have sought to reclaim a distinctly Islamic modernity and science in contrast to profane Western science. But among those Muslim applied science professionals I interviewed, I found almost unanimous objection to the very concept of Islamic science or knowledge. The generally negative view about such a prospect clearly confirmed Stenberg's finding (2000) that the effort to "Islamize" science has not reached far beyond a small circle of philosophers and theologians.

Salman, the computer science doctoral student, said, "A lot of people talk about [the Islamicization of knowledge] and reviving Islamic civilization. They want to be living in the past glory of Islam, but they have no clue as to how this past glory actually developed. Islam is a guiding principle. For instance, it brings a moral principle to the financial system, such as banking. But there are not these two separate realms [of Eastern and Western science]." Shabir, a computer programmer for a travel company who is from Pakistan, said that for Muslim and non-Muslim alike, "science is science; it's fulfilling a requirement that we contribute to humanity." Science is thus viewed as a limited instrument with a set of universal principles and techniques that are the same regardless of who practices it. Segregating science into Islamic and non-Islamic categories would, in effect, deny the universal and objective qualities of the Koran and Islam. The Koran may foreshadow and validate scientific concepts and discoveries, but these professionals also have a stake in the global science discourse and practice dispensed by its American center through universities, research institutes, and corporations.

That my small sample's views on Islam and science may reflect a broader reality can be seen in a study of scientists from Muslim and non-Muslim nations (with the majority in Southeast Asia) regarding their use of Koran-derived solutions to scientific problems. The study by Huff (1999) of the scientific discourse of natural and applied scientists found somewhat unexpectedly that it was the latter—specifically engineers—who were less likely (by 26 percent) to draw on Islamic themes in their analyses of social, economic and scientific problems and more likely to take a pragmatic approach to such questions. In contrast, it was the Muslim physicists and other natural scientists who were the most likely to take on metaphysical questions in their work, in some cases even denying the principle of causality.

Most interviewees agreed that there was an Islamic "golden age" of scientific innovation in the Middle Ages that shaped Western science, but that this was a long time ago. The frequent citations of the advanced scientific discoveries and concepts in the Koran would mean that societies shaped by Islam would be scientifically advanced. Yet they acknowledged that their own stories of migration to the United States for advanced training and work in engineering and information technology testified to serious deficiencies in science education and employment in their predominantly Islamic nations. How did they explain this discrepancy? A majority were of the view that the reason for the Islamic countries' science lag is not because of the religion itself but due to the educational systems that do not prepare students adequately for science careers. The generally negative views of Middle Eastern governments and their corrupting influence on Islam was also applied to other areas of life, such as the fields of science education and research.

The criticism of the Middle East was often set against the innovations and sense of openness the interviewees see in the United States Salman said that "the U.S. set up an amazing capitalist system [for] science. It's open to others when it comes to science. Even with 9/11 and other changes, it's still an open country. In the Middle East, kings have kept it in their interest to keep the people uninformed; it's pretty broken. But in Iran you have some of the most advanced and outstanding universities, and in India you have [the upper] middle class, and a lot of engineers and scientists." Fatima, the thirty-six-year-old researcher in computer linguistics at an Ivy League university, went further, claiming that American Muslims will have a role in reviving science and technology in Muslim countries. "The U.S. is in the forefront of science. That's where you've got to be. Any resurgence in technology in Islamic countries has to come from the West, in the diaspora communities, though maybe also from the Gulf States."

PRACTICAL SCIENCE AND THE SPIRITUAL SEARCH

In almost all the interviews I found that work and study in the applied sciences are not only an escape from the challenges to religion and faith; they also provide a way of working these dilemmas out. This is evident in these professionals' and students' accounts of their religious lives. Most of the Muslim applied scientists followed a pattern of having religious upbringings in traditionally Islamic societies. Starting in their teen years, there was more variation, with some growing indifferent about religious practice while others becoming very strict and fervent for Islam. But it was during their college years and in emigrating to the United States, when these Muslims began to construct their own Islamic identities, often through a process of intellectual searching and inquiry that tended to downplay traditional religious authorities. To some extent, these patterns were shaped by the Islamic societies in which the interviewees were raised. Those more recently arriving in the United States were more likely to be shaped by Islamic revivalist movements in their home societies, evidenced by greater disdain for secular values and modern scientific currents, such as the theory of evolution. Of course, there were exceptions. The two Iranian interviewees from Ivy League universities, one an IT student and the other a professor of engineering, reacted strongly against the Islamic revolution in their country by embracing secularism much more than the other respondents; the latter called himself a Muslim but had given up practicing his faith by the time of the interview (therefore excluded from my sample).

Ahmed, the engineer at a New Jersey telecommunications firm, grew up in a devout Muslim home in India. But he didn't think much about the faith until he came to the United States to attend college and, as he said, "started thinking for [myself]. . . . In coming to the U.S., you are more encouraged to think freely." He gradually found that Islam and the Koran offered the "solutions" to the "negative challenges" he faced in school. It was the scientific nature of the Koran and Islamic teachings that drew Ahmed to the faith. It was the way the Koran portrayed scientific facts before Western science discovered them. He pointed to algorithms, embryology (i.e., how the Koran portrays the stages of embryonic development) and the shape of the moon as examples of how the Koran has foreshadowed discoveries by modern science. Ahmed said that such consistency between God, the Koran and science testified to God's "non-contradictory nature and his ability to foretell things that are discovered now."

For Ahmed, once these concepts "clicked" for him, the "whole system [of Islam] made sense, both for the individual and the society at large." At first Ahmed made it sound as if he derived this understanding directly from his personal reading of the Koran. But in asking him about it again in a later e-mail communication, he replied that the Islamic literature he was reading at the time pointed him toward this scientific reading of the sacred text. After my interview with him at his mosque, Ahmed gave me tracts from a display rack expounding on similar Islamic-science themes. While the arguments that Islam is a particularly scientific religion may find its strongest resonance among these Muslim technoscience professionals, the discourse has spread to many other segments of the Islamic world today; it is common for Muslim websites and forums to feature science sections with articles proclaiming technological and scientific breakthroughs from the Koran (see, for example, Suyuti 2007; Rainer 2006).

Even those who showed a disinclination to mix science and Islam too freely still approached the faith in a manner that blended scientific inquiry and personal seeking. Salman, the twenty-eight-year-old computer science doctoral student, also grew up in a middle-class Muslim home in India. His father read a lot and was very religious, yet he didn't go to the mosque. "His faith was more political than spiritual," Salman recalled. He described himself growing up as a "hot-headed teen," fervently Muslim in a Hindu country. But when going to Singapore to attend college and traveling to other countries, he started taking a more intellectual approach to religion. "In meeting and listening to other people, I began to ask myself 'What if I am wrong?' Today, although he follows basic Islamic practices and teachings, Salman finds it difficult to discuss things with orthodox Muslims. "I have very strong views so it can cause problems," he said. He adheres to Islam because of its emphasis "on the oneness of God. It's very simple and dogma-free religion. It's also very logical and compelling. The Koran says open your mind and reflect on things."

Fatima, the researcher in computational linguistics, said she grew up in a "moderate Muslim" home in Egypt. She never stopped practicing the faith but in college, where she minored in philosophy, she started entertaining more doubts and questions about her beliefs. In coming to the United States for graduate study, however, she found herself becoming more defensive about Islam. She eventually became more "steady" in her religious beliefs and practice and credits her experience in the United States for giving her a mature faith. "I feel more spiritual in the U.S. because I had to find a way of clinging to the faith—you're away from the center of gravity." She is not a regular participant in one particular mosque, and credits a Koran study group with friends as helping to sustain her faith. For Fatima, that meant retaining a moderate approach to such questions as wearing the head covering, or "hijab." She continues not to wear a head covering, believing that it is not a requirement of her faith. "I'm not against it. It's not denigrating to women. If you can achieve modesty [without the head covering], that's the goal."

Seeking and finding an authentic Islamic faith also included a practical element that could make room for a therapeutic approach to spirituality. While almost all of the interviewees cited their faith in giving them motivation to work hard and achieve moral and professional excellence, some spoke from within a modern psychological-business management framework.

For example, Tariq, the Egyptian-American computer science professor in a business college, extolled the five-times-a-day call to prayer mainly for regimenting his day into discrete units of time that make for greater productivity. While I was interviewing him about his involvement in his local mosque, he mentioned that he occasionally speaks at special meetings. When I inquired what he speaks about, Tariq answered enthusiastically, "Tony Robbins!" referring to the popular human potential, motivational speaker. "I'm a big student of Tony Robbins," he added. "Sometimes when people go to the mosque, they have a hard time applying what they hear to their lives. Robbins simplifies things for contemporary life. His message that every day we should have some improvement is similar to the Islamic teaching of "perfection."

It may not be a coincidence that the interviewees with the strongest business connections and backgrounds also had an interest in personal growth and human potential techniques. For one thing, human potential and "spirituality-in-work" programs are a part of corporate culture today. More importantly, Islam is no longer a stranger to modern concerns with personal growth and seeking. A rising generation of upwardly mobile Muslims has gravitated to preachers who speak the language of self-discovery, meaning and fulfillment, such as Amr Khaled, a popular Egyptian "evangelist" trained as an accountant. Khaled is compared to a Christian evangelist stressing prosperity and the "feel-good optimism of Western management literature. . . . [He] doesn't present Muslim law, or sharia, as something to be imposed by an authority; rather he says it is something to be discovered on a journey of personal growth and awareness" (Shapiro 2006: 44-77). Most of the interviewees' emphasis on personal choice and seeking, even if it is expressed in rational scientific discourse, bears a strong similarity to such personal growth-business management discourse. Both styles embrace a pragmatic rather than an ideological approach to Islam, where personally discovering "what works" and "what makes sense" for the seeker trumps closed systems of the faith.

The widely held views among those I interviewed that Islam is a logical religion discovered through a process of searching and rational inquiry also tended to undercut traditional sources of authority. When asked about which sources they turn to when they have questions about Islamic doctrine and practice, few said they would approach their leaders or imams. Those who did were usually strongly involved in a particular mosque. But more often, the sources they valued were of a personal nature—friends and family back in their home countries, books, and of course, the Internet. They tended to favor writers, teachers, and websites that made room for questions and study (fitting in with the interactive nature of the Internet) within a conservative or orthodox framework, even if they flourished outside the rulings of traditional authorities. But it was also clear that the respondents themselves were the judges of which source to trust based on the criteria of logic and reason.

The plethora of Islamic websites and forums offering teaching, advice and fatwahs (Islamic rulings) was viewed as confusing, even by computer scientists. There was a general concern that, in the words of one interviewee, the Internet was "corrupted" by too many unreliable sources. Even those who used the Internet for religious purposes tended to frequent well-established sites that they deemed trustworthy, such as *Islamonline,* the Arabic site *www.sultan.org, Islamicity, Islamicweb.net*, and the website of the Council on American Islamic Relations (CAIR).

But my questions about "sources" of authority were for many interviewees a distraction from the one source to which every Muslim has equal access—the Koran. Shafiq, the fifty-two-year-old civil engineer working in nuclear power, said, "We're pretty much on our own, as long as we stay within the bonds of faith. I would not put my full faith in one person. I do my research and it's common to disagree [with the sources], especially when you get to be an educated person. We have no pope. When you are puzzled you can find the answer by going deeper. [When] you look into it, it's a very broad religion; it covers all the bases. It's clear-cut and there are few ambiguities." The idea that the Koran provides clear answers that do not rely on the interpretations of scholars and schools and other religious authorities was common. With a knowledge of Arabic (which most of the interviewees either had a knowledge of or were in the process of attaining), one could find that, in logically weighing and comparing chapters and verses, the Koran interprets itself. The notion that the Koran reveals its meaning and secrets to the diligent yet untutored student, much in the way that evangelical Christians believe the Bible interprets itself without the need of a magisterium, conflicts with the importance traditionally placed on rulings and judgments made by educated jurists (Roy 2004).

ISLAM, SOCIETY, AND POLITICS

The conflicting Islamic views on many issues today tended to convince these Muslims that while there are uncontested basics to the religion there are also many gray areas that they have to figure out for themselves. The emphasis on choice, personal conversion, and living out the faith in practical terms also shapes these Muslim professionals' ideas about Islam, social issues (such as biotechnology) and politics. The manner in which interviewees spoke of the comprehensive nature of Islam inevitably brought up political questions. For example, Ahmed spoke of the "whole system" of Islam "making sense for the individual and for society at large." In a telephone interview, I asked Ahmed more about Islam and politics in the United States; what would an Islamic society mean in America? In the first place, he answered, Muslim practices such as zakat (charity) are good for the economy and society, since such investment makes for the "social circulation of money" rather than using money just for the acquisition of things. He added that a "good individual makes for a good society . . . family values, high regard for the mother" and other Islamic values have an influence on the whole society.

On the application of Islamic law, or sharia, Ahmed said that Muslims are too bogged down in failing to "present a true picture of their religion" to worry about sharia or getting "special" privileges from the government. "We could always hope for something good, but [sharia] is irrelevant as of now." Besides, much of the "collective aspect of sharia cannot be applied in the United States Mohammad showed us that there is a style of following Islam in a non-Muslim as well as a Muslim society."

The other interviewees seemed less certain about the shape of Muslim political or social influence. Yusuf, a computer programmer originally from Pakistan, said he supports the implementation of sharia in Islamic societies. But when I asked him about the possibility of following sharia in the United States, he said he had never thought about that. Yusuf said that if there were a way to give Muslims the special privilege of following sharia in the United States, he might consider such a measure. But he added that accepting such Islamic laws would have to be voluntary; "we don't want to impose anything." Fatima, the computational linguist, was more negative about implementing sharia in the United States. "We were meant to be a minority in this country," she said. "Sharia is very nebulous. It's not something simple. Which sharia would we follow? There are several versions. The U.S. Constitution applies sharia."

Most of the interviewees also expressed support and admiration for the multiethnic and multireligious character of the United States. Fareed, a thirty-five-year-old Egyptian-born computer science student at a large state university, said he likes the fact that "people come from all different cultures and religions" in the United States. At the same time, he sees no conflict between "secular values and the Islamic religion."

If Muslim applied scientists and other professionals exert significant influence in their communities because of their educations and social status, then it might be expected that American Islam would reflect many of the tendencies and values discussed in this article. This pattern can be seen in the Pew Research Center survey of Muslim Americans (2008), which shows that Muslim immigrants are highly integrated into American society. With the exception of very recent immigrants, most reported that a large proportion of their closest friends are non-Muslims. Only young (and largely native-born and African-American) Muslims resembled European Muslims in their support of suicide bombing in some instances (one-quarter), while most foreign-born Muslim immigrants (78 percent) say suicide bombing is never justified. The varied interpretations of sharia found among my sample have also been found among Muslim populations in Western countries (Esposito 2010).

APPLIED SCIENCE AND THE DE-TRADITIONALIZING OF ISLAM

There were few signs that work in science and technology had a detrimental or secularizing effect on these professionals' Islamic faith. One could argue that the interviewees' high valuation of technology and the large degree of autonomy they granted this sphere may have a secularizing impact on how they think about American religion and society. Yet they argued that their relatively benign views of technology were well within the parameters of their faith, and was even a sign that Islam is more naturally friendly to technology and science than such a religion as Christianity.

As for the second theory—that applied science serves as an escape from the cognitive challenges posed by the social sciences and the humanities—it is the case that several Muslim professionals and students view their work and study in these fields as "safe." This was especially true for students just starting out on their career trajectory. It may be that such protection from secular or "anti-religious" ideology is a motivation in studying applied science, but over time, and once established in the profession, it will be joined with more positive approaches to the faith-work relationship. More research is needed to determine the extent to which the tendency toward value neutrality of these fields serves as a protective zone for conservative beliefs throughout the career trajectory. It can be argued that those viewing their work in engineering or computer science as a safe harbor from assaults to the faith would also arrive at a position where their work actually bolsters their beliefs and challenges the secularism they see around them. After all, the engineer or software designer is granted the privileged place of mimicking in their work the designs established by God. In other words, these professionals' faith compels them to "stand back" from their ordinary work and reconceptualize it in spiritual terms—something that would not occur in the everyday process of asking and answering scientific and technological questions by a more secular engineer (Martin 2005). Moreover, these Muslim applied scientists did not see a high degree of competition between the institutional logic of their workplace and that of Islamic life, at least as it is expressed in the American context; they believe that much of the same logic they use in everyday problem-solving at work is also applicable in finding spiritual answers and dealing with dilemmas of the faith. Contrary to Max Weber's predictions, the utilitarian worldview fostered by applied science and technology can as easily lead to re-enchantment as to disenchantment for the professionals and students in my sample. Rather than scientific work and study relegating religion to a private and marginal sphere, as Weber suggested, it is the mundane and seemingly utilitarian endeavors of science and technology that are spiritualized.

But isn't such a spiritualization of science and its relation to these professionals' unchallenged and conservative faith just another manifestation of fundamentalism? It is here that my results diverge more sharply from previous research asserting a special relationship between applied science and Islamic activism and extremism. While the institutional logic of applied science may protect and in certain ways even bolster the religious logic of Islam (i.e., the concept of God as designer), the way in which both this profession and immigrant upward mobility are configured in the American class and educational system tends to move these professionals away from an activist or Islamist ideology. If one pays attention to Muslims in the West outside of religious institutions, such as mosques or Islamic organizations, many are found to follow a pragmatic approach to their religion (Jeldtoft 2010). But the values of choice, searching, and freedom of expression encouraged by "upward assimilation" through American higher education along with immersion in the cultures of engineering and IT in the United States tend to create a more pragmatic style of religious thought that can coexist with traditional beliefs and practices. American educational and professional life provides these Muslim professionals with the social space in which, through personal searching and experimentation, they can creatively adapt and rework beliefs and practices to meet personal and professional needs. As Olivier Roy and others have shown, the drive for "authenticity" and the view that "happiness on earth fits with heavenly salvation" has become part of a "globalized Islam," though it finds special resonance in the United States (Roy 2004: 195). While it is not the case that these professionals would spurn external revelation as expressed in the Koran for internalized spiritual experiences in the way that a New Age seeker might, there is some truth to the observation that many modern believers have taken a "subjective turn," playing the role of the seeker in relation to tradition. Paul Heelas and Linda Woodhead (2009) contrast what they call "life as religion," consisting of following external rules and authority passed down from a tradition with that of "subjective-life" spirituality concerned with inner-well-being and personal experience and authenticity.

That these "de-traditionalized" sentiments are voiced by fairly recent immigrants from a tradition outside of Western Christianity is a sign that such discourse is prevalent in the United States and that it is highly adaptable and appealing to other believers. The fact that Muslims display some attraction to human potential-therapeutic techniques and teachings may be related to the self-help and subjective values of upper-middle-class American corporate culture, where there has been a merging of an externally-driven Protestant work ethic with internalized motivational self-help and human potential techniques (Miller 2007).

The relationship between religion and work and study in science and technology involves a process of interaction where professionals and students use an amalgam of (not always orthodox) scientific and religious logics to both reaffirm and reshape their faith. An examination of a larger sample of Muslim applied scientists from outside of the New York area, with its large and dense Muslim population, could substantiate my findings on a wider scale. A comparison of Muslim applied science professionals in different societies, as well as a study of Muslims and non-Muslims in different occupations, could illuminate the significance of the institutional logic of applied science in influencing religious discourse.

In discussing the religiosity of young Americans, Robert Wuthnow (2007) finds that they engage in "spiritual tinkering." This is where available ideas, practices and beliefs are pieced together "from the materials at hand," whether they come from partially recalled Sunday school lessons, conversations with friends, television programs, or websites. Wuthnow contrasts this improvisational approach with "religious professionals who approach spirituality the way an engineer might construct a building." But I found that even engineers do a certain amount of "tinkering" as they construct a religious identity. A mixture of applied, theoretical, orthodox and non-orthodox science provided the tools for these professionals to engage in a religious search, even if it was more often confined to the firm borders of their tradition rather than encompassing the vast religious marketplace. Like the spiritual seeker tinkering for available resources, these professionals did not accept their traditions wholesale but rather enlisted the tools and logics at hand, those of practicality and empirical truth-seeking, as they constructed their religious lives and discourse. Of course, such searching could move in so-called "liberal," "moderate," or "conservative" directions. But for the Muslim professional and student interviewees, the scientific values of experimentation, empiricism and the American immigrant quest for upward mobility often led to a subjective turn that moderated the objective demands of Islam as well broadening out into a more pragmatic approach to social and political matters.

There is nothing inevitable about science professionals and students interacting with religion in pragmatic directions. These professions carry the potential of accommodating various religious orientations. Even proponents of the view that a universal "engineering mindset" is in sync with Islamic militancy, such as Gambetta and Hertog (2009), acknowledge the powerful role of occupational and national contexts in such a formation. The outcome depends on the institutional and religious logics that are brought to bear on one's work and study.

Chapter Two

Rationalized Hinduism and Mystical Science

The mysticism and ritualism of Hinduism seem a world apart from the precise and pragmatic precincts of engineering and computer science. Yet the diffuse and diverse religion of Hinduism has long adapted itself to new forms of knowledge. The Hindu teaching that its body of scriptures, known as the Vedas, encompasses all forms of knowledge easily accommodates the sciences, even if not of the most orthodox lineage. In this chapter, I find that the Hindu entrance into these professions does not necessarily result in secularization or a loss of religious vitality, but it does lead to new interactions that change both religious and scientific discourse.

Research shows that both sending and receiving nations are key to understanding how immigrant career trajectories are channeled among Indian Hindus. In the case of the latter, many of the migrant workers arriving in the United States after 1965 (when immigration law was expanded to include many non-Europeans) were born into India's urban, professional middle classes, preparing themselves for "out-migration years in advance by seeking out particular kinds of higher education, professional training, or investment opportunities that will maximize their access to student or immigrant visas. . . . By this time, prospective arrivals can tap into well-established employment and educational networks both in India and the United States" (Lessinger 2001). By the 1970s, India had created a large network of schools for scientific research and education (such as the Indian Institute of Technology, or IIT) and subsequently a large pool of labor willing to work in the West. In the 1980s and 1990s, India itself had developed economically to offer technology and science jobs to its people. The growth of a technology sector in India and a growing diaspora of science professionals abroad created new economic and cultural networks that transcended national boundaries (Chakravartty 2000).

The software boom in India and the growth of the applied sciences in general have been associated with the development of a new Hindu consciousness as well. Thus in Banglore, India's Silicon Valley, it is not unusual for even Hindu rituals to be carried out in software firms (Tulasi 2002). The enormous growth of the software industry in India in the 1980s moved beyond the usual pocket of elite schools and educational professionals in the major metropolises (mainly on the coasts) and reached into the hinterlands. The form of Hindu religiosity more prevalent in small towns and villages was joined with "neo-Hindu ideology" and high-tech culture, providing a way for these workers to become modern while still holding on to familiar signs of authority (Rajagopal 2000).

TECHNOSCIENCE DISCOURSE AND HINDUISM

In my interviews with Hindu applied science professionals, I found a persistent concern to relate their faith to scientific progress. Most of them stressed that Hinduism is the "most scientific religion" since it involves the continuous search for truth. Rajiv, a recently retired computer science and management professor, said that in Hinduism "the mind is always evolving. In Christianity and Islam, either you accept it or you don't; you can't ask questions. They have the Bible and Koran complete and don't add anything. Hinduism is open to knowledge. In Hinduism they're always writing new [sacred texts]."

Some of the respondents described their faith as more suitable to modern American society and its high valuation of science than that of evangelical and fundamentalist Christians. The retired computer science professor said the United States is renowned for its science and if "that's lost, everything is. I'm worried about the growth and influence of evangelicals," and how they may reverse the scientific and technological advances in the United States With few exceptions, most saw the growth of technology as largely beneficial, even on controversial issues involving biotechnology, such as stem cell research (although there was some concern among more orthodox Hindus that cloning may violate God's design). This tendency to be tolerant and flexible on bioethical issues surrounding technology is not unique to these Hindu applied scientists in the United States. In fact, India's emerging role as a center of biotechnology research and therapy has been attributed to its Hindu culture and its non-dogmatic, pragmatic approach to such issues (Sachdev 2006).

A HINDU WORK ETHIC?

The non-dogmatic and pragmatic approach to technology and science of these applied science professionals was also evident in the way they related their faith to their everyday work lives. They did not report many significant ethical dilemmas or contradictions between their religion and their work in engineering and information technology. While some said that their faith did serve as a support for rational or logical thinking on the job, it was mainly seen as a source of motivation for hard work and a way of dealing with the inevitable failures and setbacks they encountered in their careers.

Myuran, a retired systems engineer from Westchester, said that his faith helps him to "carry out your duty, to do the right thing and not worry about the results. Even if the results don't work out, you don't give up, no matter what the consequences." Fulfilling one's duty was closely linked with karma, the deeds and results in the process of reincarnation. In a cause-and-effect relationship, a bad thing that happens would be the result of misdeeds in one's previous life. This can lead both to an acceptance of misfortune but also a chance of improving one's lot and future lives by producing good karma. Cultivating the spirituality it takes to accept one's karma and to "do one's duty," usually through meditation, was viewed as reducing stress and increasing well-being on the job.

"Doing the right thing" was often defined by being honest and fair in one's dealings with co-workers and clients. For Rajiv, the retired computer science and management professor, Hindu ethics have influenced him most in his teaching and views on hiring and firing practices. "It's an indecent capitalism that fires people after years of giving their lives to their companies. You have to show some respect for the work and the worker." One finds in popular Hindu literature and publications, often written by those in business and applied science, the concept that work is a form of worship; which was echoed among some of the interviewees who said that one's house or workplace can be as holy as a temple. An article by a computer engineering professor in *Hinduism Today* magazine puts it provocatively: "I approach my job every morning with the thought that I am going to the 'Temple of Electrical and Computer Engineering,' where I will workship. The first thing I do when I enter my office is offer salutations to the statue of Lord Ganesha, which I have installed in a small shrine there. Then I go to workship with my staff, students and faculty colleagues, striving always to carry out my tasks with a willpower born of the conviction that for 'every problem, there is not just a solution, but a good solution'" (Rao 2005).

AT THE INTERSECTION OF WESTERN AND EASTERN SCIENCE

In some cases, the science valued by these professionals took several detours from conventional science. Science derived from the Vedas (for example, Vedic mathematics) was seen as complementing and making more comprehensive Western science. During my interview with Sanjay, a fifty-one-year-old computer programmer, he showed me a painting of a Hindu saint and told me that he has lived for three hundred years, and that there were some saints who reached a state of perfection and have lived for as many as three thousand years. When I remarked that most scientists would have problems with that claim, he first replied that many of the techniques and "sciences" of Hinduism, such as Ayuveda, have since been confirmed by Western scientists. But he added, "You have to use reason; reason brings you to the edge of the springboard and then you have to take the leap of faith." But this programmer was educated in business and was a true autodidact both in science and religion. Those trained in the applied sciences were more likely to stress the congruence between their religion and Western science.

A small number did claim that Hinduism is strictly a spiritual system that had nothing to do with science. Jagdish, a computer programmer with the police department, came from a Brahmin and Saivite (Hinduism dedicated to the deity Shiva and largely based in South India) home where his father was a Sanskrit scholar. The more time he spent in the temple as a child, the more interested he became in Hinduism. In coming to the United States as a college student, Jagdish became less devout. It was only after taking up meditation as a practice that he became more involved in the Hindu community. Today, he volunteers at the temple, as well as practices pujas (Hindu rituals) and prayers at home. The way in which Hinduism is sometimes seen as a cultural or social identity is disturbing to Jagdish. "Religion is religion; it's not a social thing," he said. He expresses the same ambivalence about making connections between his faith and his work. Hinduism helps him realize the transitory nature of things, including success, and puts him in a "good frame of mind in dealing with problems." But he sees little crossover between spiritual and scientific or technical knowledge. "There's material knowledge and there's spiritual knowledge—they don't have anything to do with each other. No amount of computer science will bring peace of mind; only meditation can do that. . . . Religion is a faith while science tries to prove something. At some point science breaks down."

More typical is Myuran, the retired Westchester systems engineer, who said that he values Hinduism because "logic is not shunned and discouraged. Science and religion are both the same—it's the search for truth. . . . What the saints did five thousand years ago, science is doing now. It's the same track." Rajiv, the retired computer science and management professor, explained this concept further when he spoke of Hinduism as a philosophy that served as a "cover" for science throughout the ages. For instance, the scientific theory of the big bang, when all the chemical elements emerged from hydrogen, was foreshadowed by the Hindu concept that the world is one and everything came from a divine source and is returning to that source. "Religion is full of science but in an abstract way," he added.

Vijay, a forty-two-year-old computer programmer at a chemical plant in New Jersey, viewed the existence of supernatural spirits and miracles through the perspective of science. He has been taught that there are three ways of knowing the truth—scriptures, the guru, and experience. "If experience goes against the other two then it's not truth for me," he said. "For example, I have doubts about the spirits. The scriptures [teach about them], but I still doubt. I'm skeptical about claims for miracles. These things we don't understand . . . have to be reconciled through science—that's how we'll understand it; that's God's mechanism of truth."

The account of Narayana, a sixty-two-year-old engineer and consultant, suggests the attraction of a scientific approach to Hinduism among these professionals. He was raised in a Brahmin family that he said was "spiritual but not religious." In India "the problem is that most Hindus are more religious than spiritual; they're following rituals blindly without knowing what they're doing." In middle school in India he started studying the Bhagavadgita and throughout his engineering studies and career, he has remained "knowledge-driven . . . I don't practice anything blindly; I have an insatiable desire to learn and decipher things. I don't need priests [to explain Hindu teachings]. I have a clear understanding." Today, he is more conventionally religious, occasionally attending temple, keeping in touch with a guru, and practicing rituals, such as reciting morning prayers and chanting, mainly because he "understands their meaning." He said that a "knowledge of science helps people understand spirituality more than such fields as the arts and commerce. . . . In the material life, science is helpful in understanding spirituality faster. You can't accept theologies blindly or believe for belief's sake. But people coming from other backgrounds, such as the arts, may accept certain doctrines blindly. This is what's happened in the rest of the world's religions."

But he added that those scientists who "follow the material life" and discount such occurrences as miracles are "ignorant." Those scientists, however, who have both "material knowledge and spiritual knowledge, can see things more clearly." In a similar way, he called the theories of Darwinian evolution "all humbug" because they deny the universe's infinite existence. He is certain that such theories will eventually be disproven from a "logical" perspective.

The engineers I interviewed particularly viewed the practical and applied nature of their science as challenging—independent of their Hindu faith—the theoretical sciences. Krishna, an engineering professor, criticized scientists for their tendency to do research without being responsible for their results. "In engineering you have to know the possible results beforehand. For instance, will [the results of the research] be biodegradable? Many scientists don't take responsibility and see religious people as obstructing [their work]." Vidya, a computer programmer who was trained as an engineer in India, expressed his doubts about Darwinian evolution from an engineering perspective. He said that "scientists deal with probability, saying something like evolution has a probability of taking place. For the engineer, it would be a very minute possibility, but it's not likely. I don't care if [it works] on a piece of paper, the engineer has to make it happen." He added that he is more inclined to accept "intelligent design" (though he has never read intelligent design literature), mainly because the concept of design makes more sense to an engineer's mind. In the same way, he argued that such advances in biotechnology as cloning violate nature's original design. While most of the interviewees accepted some form of evolution, the Vedic teaching on the infinite nature of the universe caused some uneasiness about Darwinian concepts of the origins of the earth. The conflation of spiritual evolution with biological evolution has been a staple of Hindu literature on science since the colonial period, with such writings tending to downplay if not dismiss natural and random selection theories prominent in Darwinism (Brown 2012).

During my interview with Sanjay, the fifty-one-year-old computer programmer, he reached into his bag and produced an article from a website in order to explain the teachings of his faith. What was most revealing was how the essay was framed around an applied sciences and technological mindset. It stated that the "world is becoming more digital in all respects. Everything needs to be presented in black and white for acceptance. Grey is no more an option in many cases. In olden days, such clarity was required only in scientific matters. But today no one is willing to accept anything that is illogical and insipid. Matters of faith are no exception. People are looking for clear definitions and meanings in all rituals and beliefs . . . the distinguishing pillars of each faith need to be highlighted in this highly competitive field. Each of us have [sic] to list out the USP (Unique Selling Propositions) of our faith to satisfy others and ourselves."

The author then proceeds to describe Hinduism as only an engineer can. "Hypothetically, we are building up a structure on the firm ground of reason to reach a certain point in space. The most stable structure is a dome and that is what Hi-Faith [the author's term for Hinduism] is. It can be said that a dome has an infinite number of pillars but here we will search for the salient pillars that distinguish it from others." After listing five pillars for Hinduism, he concludes that the "most progressive feature of Hi-Faith is its 100 percent compatibility with Science, especially the modem variety wherein we reach the conclusion that everything is just Maya and the truth is only one" (Kumar 2005). The interactive nature of the Internet itself adds to the democratic yet standardized discourse produced by technoscience professionals. Thus, directly after this article, another writer adds several "additional pillars" to delineate his conception of "authentic" Hinduism.

The discourse cited above has spread far from its base among applied scientists. An article in the popular magazine *Hinduism Today* carries a remarkably similar article, though written by a guru. In calling for a "user-friendly presentation of Hinduism," author Satguru Bodhinatha Veylanswami writes that "teachings and practices that were once accepted without question are often now rejected unless evidence and logic are marshaled to give them plausibility. To survive, customs and traditions must bear up under intellectual scrutiny, must prove themselves helpful and immediately useable" (Veysanswami 2007).

The attempt to categorize or "pillarize" Hinduism in the United States is not entirely unique to applied scientists. In a religious tradition as diffuse and complex as Hinduism that has been transplanted into a society with little knowledge of its teachings and practices, it is not surprising to find several attempts to craft a simplified articulation of the religion in order to explain it to outsiders (Eck 2000). But the very act of categorizing and classifying bears a special affinity to scientific and rationalized methods of thinking common to applied science professionals.

Gyan Prakesh (1999) notes that the reliance on empirical science to establish and explain the truth of Hinduism, an endeavor that first flourished in late-nineteenth-century India, conflicts with the older Sanskritic traditions asserting that Vedic truths are transcendent and need no confirmation. This form of scientific Hinduism was clearly espoused by Sidra, a thirty-two-year-old mechanical engineering professor at a technical college in Brooklyn. Unlike the other Hindu professionals I interviewed, Sidra saw no value at all in Hindu rituals and has been largely uninvolved in Hindu institutional life since arriving in the United States for graduate study seven years ago. For him the religion began and ends in science. "Hinduism started from science. The first question in the Vedas is 'Where Does the earth come from?' A lot of our knowledge in mathematics, physics and astronomy come straight out of the Vedas. Later on, the priests started dominating and the religion became corrupt. Religious leaders took control of society. Natural powers [came to be seen] as gods. The gods were made by the priests. . . . Until science gives us explanations, we tend to call [unexplained phenomenon] God." Sidra conceded that eventually all supernatural beliefs may be explained by science. Yet he says he is a strong believer in God and values Hinduism for teaching the "purity of body and thought and that one should remember God in good times, not only in bad."

The above accounts clearly demonstrate how these professionals' discourse on Hinduism has become highly rationalized and subjected to the standards of meaning, practical logic, and empiricism. The tendency of separating Hindu spirituality from its rituals and communal expressions (expressed in the maxim, "I'm spiritual but not religious") and the distilling of the vast body of Hindu tradition and scriptures into basic "pillars" are modem innovations that are found across the religious spectrum from East to West, taking up a globalized expression.

But rationalization does not come in one form, nor does it always mean a pillarization or standardization of the faith on utilitarian grounds. This could be seen in the case of Krishna, another mechanical engineering professor at a prestigious technical university. Krishna is a renaissance man as well as what Max Weber would call a "religious virtuoso"; he runs dramatic productions for his university and is an expert Sanskrit scholar, and an accomplished author, speaker, and guru on Hinduism. His faith is firmly embedded in the rituals of the temple. Krishna has developed what he calls a program of "multi-faceted Vedic Hinduism," where his background in engineering is no less evident than it is for his colleague Sidra, though in dramatically different form. He presented a many-layered tradition consisting of rituals, art, music, mantras, yoga and meditation, as well as science and philosophical systems. Each component, built upon Dharma or principles of life, has its function in awakening and sustaining spiritual knowledge and life. A specialist in acoustics, Krishna includes intricate diagrams in his writings of the value and mechanics of sound and how chanting and the use of the conch shell channel the "spiritual vibrations" of the universal sound OM. Far from trying to break down religion into basic pillars, Krishna argues that Vedic Hinduism integrates the arts, sciences, and the social and religious dimensions. There is also, of course, an overview of the technological and scientific contributions of Vedic Hinduism, from the concept and use of zero and the decimal system to developments in metallurgy.

It is also the case that the Hindu applied science discourse I heard drew heavily on the New Age movement. When I inquired about the Hindu perspective on science I was often referred to the 2004 popular film, *What The Bleep Do We Know*. This is a documentary on quantum physics and reality that espouses what could be considered a New Age or holistic perspective on the nature of reality. That there was an affinity to Hinduism could be seen in the film's citing of the Uphanishads and Hindu gurus, though it just as frequently presented the ideas of the New Age spirit "channeller" Ramtha and the spiritual musings of Albert Einstein. Such concepts as the oneness and eternal nature of the universe, the immanence of God in creation, and the linkage between internal spiritual enlightenment achieved through spiritual disciplines (such as yoga) and the spiritual harmony of the outside world and universe all lend themselves to frequent New Age–Hindu exchanges and borrowing. Of course, the Hindu would argue that the New Age movement has only appropriated original Hindu concepts. Yet the application of Hindu concepts to business and corporate life, as well as to science, has borrowed significantly from the New Age and human potential movements (D. Miller 2007). The Hindu references to New Age resources suggest that they benefit as much from such borrowings as their Western counterparts, lending their teachings an American legitimacy and popularity, even as such ideas find a global audience.

Thus we see that rationalization can be expressed very differently. What these different forms have in common is the attempt to make Hinduism understandable and legitimate in scientific and rational terms. Just how such an affinity between rationalized Hinduism and applied science may be "elective" and not bound to this professional strata will be discussed in the next section.

HINDU APPLIED SCIENCE PROFESSIONALS IN THEIR RELIGIOUS COMMUNITIES

Rajiv, the retired computer science and management professor, is a man of serious, even intense, bearing who does not wear his learning lightly. During our interview, he was not hesitant to offer me unsolicited, rapid-fire advice on everything from the fine points of hydrogen fusion to matters of diet and sexuality, intermittingly quizzing me to make sure I understood. I interviewed him in the temple's canteen, which served non-stop rounds of Indian meals as worshippers made their way to and from the temple. Everyone seemed to know Rajiv; when I had told the temple's president that I was to interview him, she raised her eyebrows and suppressed a brief laugh, hinting that I was in for an experience. Rajiv came to the temple every weekend, both to worship and to circulate around the book counter in the canteen and offer customers advice and suggestions about the Hindu literature on display. In many ways he was similar to the older Hindus I met who took up spiritual and religious interests in their retirement and semi-retirement. The Hindu tradition teaches that the later stages of life—when many have taken vows of renunciation—should focus on spiritual and ascetic concerns.

Rajiv, seventy, grew up in South India in a Brahmin family and graduated from the prestigious India Institute of Technology and Engineering (ITE) in Bombay. He is devout but doesn't see much of the ritual or even the Hindu community itself as very important. If the temple caught fire tomorrow, "it wouldn't change things. I can do [the rituals] in my house. This assembly is for people who don't go [to] the second level of religion. Spirituality is more important than ritual." As on a host of other subjects, Rajiv viewed himself as being "self-taught in religion." He admits that he sometimes feels like a "misfit" in Hinduism, since he is very individualistic. He would consult gurus and priests, but the problem is that he "can't find many that know more" than him. He relies on visits to the library and the Internet to learn more about Hinduism.

Rajiv sees it as his vocation to work with younger IT professionals, whom he says have largely lost their Hindu beliefs and values. "Indians as a whole are becoming too materialistic. The young tech workers I have worked and spoken with are attracted by divorce." He believes technology can be destructive of Hindu values and that it has to be used properly, even as he sees science as the most important force in the United States.

There was a clear autodidactic tendency when it comes to religion among most of the Hindu applied science professionals I interviewed. There was variation in the level of religious observance and practice among the interviewees; some never went to the Hindu temple and had a low rate of religious practice (such as meditation and enacting rituals), while others showed a good deal of communal, ritual, and personal religious commitment. The temple structure seems to lend itself to such internal pluralism. Worshippers come and go, even while the punja or prayer service is being chanted by the priests. Devotees of one particular deity who may gather in one comer of the temple can rub shoulders but have little else to do with those venerating another god or goddess elsewhere.

Even in the canteen, the loose-fitting nature of Hinduism was on display. Rajiv and his friends at the book counter openly argued and disputed Hindu teachings and practice, showing little concern that the temple president and other officials were within earshot. Sidha, who volunteers his weekends to work behind the book counter, admitted that he never goes to the temple next door to worship. Instead, he goes to meditation sessions at the Center for the Art of Living, an interfaith yoga and meditation movement. He was raised in a devout Brahmin home, but between the ages of fifteen and twenty-five considered himself an atheist. He studied at ITE in Bombay, taking graduate degrees in physics and computer science. In the United States, he started becoming more religious after watching Wayne Dyer, a human potential and spiritual teacher, on Public Television. Sidha views the main effects of his faith on his work as creating a "peaceful state" of mind. The spiritualized Hinduism as represented by the Center for the Art of Living widely appeals to IT professionals in India and abroad. The success of this movement, based in Banglore, India's Silicon Valley, is "closely connected to the emergence of the information technology industry as one of the vital elements of India's 'opening up' for the world market," according to Peter van der Veer (2014: 192). The center runs courses targeted to the business world and especially IT professionals, mainly centered on its meditation and breathing techniques to help deal with the stress that comes from a hectic workload (Amrute 2010).

When I met with the temple president, a retired gynecologist and obstetrician, at the time of my interviews with these professionals, she was annoyed but not surprised about the relaxed attitude many take toward formal religious observance, "You can worship anywhere in Hinduism, but in the temples you find the [spiritual] vibrations [coming from] the pujas and chanting tremendous. . . . There are dogmas behind the spirituality which forms the base or the foundation [of the faith]." As much as the temple president may not like it, most of the interviewees tended to emphasize learning and selecting Hindu teachings for oneself without the mediation of religious authorities. Myuran, the retired systems engineer, writes and speaks often on Hindu topics, but the only times he enters a Hindu temple is to teach a class of children. "I go [to the temple] to teach and do social work. I tell the priests, 'you guys do what you do and I'll teach.'" He is particularly critical of the swamis who seek to transmit Hindu teachings to Americans. "About 99 percent of them don't know English [and] can't relate to [children]. . . . I want to speak to the children from what I know. I want to create the curiosity for them to learn on their own. I feel a responsibility to impart their heritage to them and then leave them free to believe what they want." Only a small number agreed that they would consult a priest or guru if they had a particular dilemma or question regarding Hinduism. One computer programmer did say he regularly consults his guru at the Hindu temple, but his guru is an engineering professor who translates many of his teachings into scientific lingo.

I originally approached this research thinking that Hindu engineers and computer scientists represented an elite that held most of the positions of power within Hindu temples and organizations (Zaidman 2000). While such organizational clout may be the case in some temples, particularly on the West Coast (in Silicon Valley, in particular), in the New York–New Jersey area the boards of directors and other leadership positions were usually occupied by medical doctors and those working in finance. Despite his rounds at the temple's canteen, Rajiv had just lost the temple elections for a seat on the board and complained that doctors typically gained such positions because they were more adept at publicizing themselves and campaigning in the community.

Very few of the applied science professionals I interviewed were in positions of temple leadership, but most taught classes (both to adults and children) and several lectured on Hinduism outside the temple (such as to interfaith groups), as well as discussed and wrote on Hinduism on the Internet. Thus these applied scientists have considerable impact on the representation and dissemination of Hindu teachings to fellow members (as well as to those outside the community), if not through the organizational and ritual dimensions of Hinduism.

The influence that these professionals have on an intellectual and educational level may well serve to generalize their rationalized discourse to the wider Hindu community. As Weber noted, the religious content produced by one social stratum can be adopted to meet the needs of other strata. It is true that Weber holds that intellectuals are able to transcend their class interests more than other social strata and tend to produce knowledge for those of other classes (Weber 1946). But these technoscience professionals' work in practical rather than theoretical knowledge, which, as mentioned earlier, could place them in the civil strata. This would make for a unique case, with these professionals possibly extending their influence in several directions—among the "masses" as well as among intellectuals. As noted above, the rationalized discourse of these Hindu professionals is evident in the national and international Hindu media, such as the magazine *Hinduism Today,* with its frequent references to the scientific and practical nature of the religion. The emphasis one finds on Hindu principles of management and instilling a Hindu work ethic in such literature can be found among both applied science and financial professionals (see, for example, Rao, 2005).

In my fieldwork, the influence of such professionals was not very evident in the large and pluralistic urban temple in New York, which tended to feature orthodox devotional literature based on the Hindu scriptures, for children as well as adults, at its book counters. But such influence was more visible at a smaller temple I visited in a New Jersey suburb. After attending a class on Hindu teachings taught by an engineering professor, I was told that I should stay for a lecture by a renowned swami, who also happened to be an engineer before he renounced his secular life and took up monastic vows.

Book tables in the social hall where the lecture was to take place were stacked with copies of the Vedas and the Bhagavadgita alongside glossy booklets and tracts with such titles as "Personnel Management," "Action and Reaction," "Need for Cognitive Change," and "Freedom from Sadness." The lecture was likewise aimed at professionals who were seeking spiritual solace and practical direction amid their busy lives. "You can have all the knowledge about the world and have two degrees," the Swami intoned, switching between English and Hindi. "Having all knowledge is great but it doesn't solve the basic problem. . . . You are the cause of your problems with other people."

HINDU CULTURE AND POLITICS VERSUS SPIRITUALITY

As with Muslim applied scientists, there have been several attempts to link the Hindu presence in the IT industry to the growth of Hindu fundamentalism. Scholarly literature has tended to view upward mobile and technologically astute professionals as the vehicle through which Hindu nationalism has spread throughout the Indian diaspora. It is the most recent wave of immigrant IT professionals (such as those coming to the United States to work on Y2K issues before the new millennium) who were trained in the new computer programming schools and came from a wider spread of small cities and towns in the Indian hinterland who are portrayed as being conflicted, alienated, and "dispossessed" of their own Hindu and Indian history and identity. Biju Mathew and Vijay Prashad write that these migrants "who live in isolated, chiefly Euro-American, suburbs" have a "heightened alarm at the possibility of 'Americanization'" (Mathew and Prashad 2000). These individuals are recruited to the Hindu nationalist cause by such organizations as the Hindu Swayamsevak Sangh, the Vishwa Hindu Parshad of America (VHP) or even the Hindu Student Council, which run special programs and camps to appeal to IT professionals, according to Mathew and Prashad. In one ethnographic study of such a camp cited by Rajagopal (2000), where prayers and seminars are tailored to participants' interests, an "Upanishadic management consultant spoke to an avid crowd of engineers, applying the insights of the Upanishads to management."

These techno-professionals are said to form the financial backbone for many of these revivalist Hindu groups, both donating and engaging in fundraising drives for causes in the United States and in India. It is the case that the majority of the interviewees said they have supported a variety of causes and groups in India, usually of a religious nature. Some of the younger professionals said they wanted to eventually return to India. But this may speak more of the transnational nature of immigrant life today than involvement in a specific ideology (Levitt 2007). According to critics of the Hindu right, it is particularly on the Internet where the technoscience professionals have fueled their fundamentalist fervor. On such well-funded websites of the Hindu right as the Global Hindu Electronic Network, an inquirer finds "packaged information . . . and artifacts of Hindu culture, such as a database of Indian names and a collection of articles, all dealing with the question, Who is a Hindu?" Mathew and Prashad (2000) write that the text of such sites is "fragmented into a set of hypotheses, axioms, assumptions and 'facts.'" Questions and challenges about Indian history in such forums are "mounted by Indian professionals of a science and technology background, who express open distrust for the methods of historians and who are convinced that they are better equipped by the positivist traditions of science to make decisive assertions about Indian history."

Of these professionals, Mathew and Prashad (2000) write: "For about two hours each day, many male Indian professionals surf the Net and converse with other Indian men, talk nostalga, talk spiritual, talk India. They all share a language developed in their years in elite and semi-elite technical institutions—a language with a unique tenor of scientific arrogance, one that is honed with witty metaphors of subtle racism, homophobia, and sexism." The writers see the technological professionals' involvement with such Hindu groups as providing them with an "inventory of isolated cultural packets that work successfully as symbolic capital" in resisting Americanization. They add that "in the isolation of the Internet, scores of technical-professional migrants washed away the stain of their corporate existence by exercising a jingoistic nationalism." The postmodern and postcolonialist left targets the Hindu right for its use of positivist and Western science to legitimize native Hindu and Indian traditions.

But perhaps the sharpest criticism of the Hindu right's appropriation of science has come from Indian secular rationalists. Meera Nanda (2003) throws cold water on the whole enterprise of Hindus (and particularly nationalists) finding scientific concepts and roots in the Vedas and Hindu traditions, arguing that "scientific developments in India took place not because of, but in spite of the philosophical idealism of the Vedantic orthodoxy." Science as it developed in the Enlightenment necessitates a "delimiting" of God (from the political realm, for instance) and a disenchantment of nature, according to Nanda. Such differentiations have taken place in Western religions, as evidenced in the separation of church and state and in the autonomy of the scientific from religious spheres, but are impossible within the holistic system of Hinduism, she argues.

But as my interviews and recent research suggest, the lines between the immigrant technical professional class and Hindu nationalism, as well as between "Hindu science" and Western science, are not very straight nor clear. With few exceptions, the interviewees accepted Western science as "modem" and global, even if they disputed its origins and sought spiritual meanings to scientific phenomena in a similar manner as do Western Christians. The concern for greater spirituality and less ritualism evident among several interviewees can move in various directions—from ruling out politics as a distraction to affirming such activism as a means to secure Hindu (and thus spiritual) rights and identity in India. For instance, Narayana, the sixty-two-year-old engineer, said he is not involved or interested in Indian politics, but in his concern about how ritualism has overtaken spirituality, he uses nationalist rhetoric about how first Muslim and then British rule has distorted authentic Hinduism in its native land. As with many other "non-political" interviewees, Narayana was of the view that the Hindu majority is deprived of its rights as the government has made special provisions for Christian and particularly Muslim minorities. This concern with the natural rights of Hindus in India often clashed with the strong interfaith and multicultural views about the United States expressed by most interviewees (Narayana was baptized as a Christian and worships and speaks in churches in the United States while maintaining his Hindu identity).

Pandit, a forty-five-year-old civil engineer, was raised in Gujarat in the Vaisyaya (or commerce-based) caste. His family had a special devotion to the gods Vishnu and Shiva, though in his teen years he tried to be "modern" and distanced himself from his faith. Today, he practices yoga and attends a class on Hindu teachings, but goes to the temple more for his children than his own religious needs. Because of his busy schedule and the social obligations associated with the business he runs, Pandit eats meat and drinks alcohol. "It's a compromise, though [following such rules] are not as significant as much as helping others," he said. After establishing his business, Pandit would like to go back to India and do more concerning "self-searching and spirituality." Along with his growing interest in the spiritual teachings and practices of Hinduism, he has become increasingly agitated about the loss of Hindu identity in India. He believes that Hindus are "victimized" by Muslims in India. "The Muslims bother the hell out of me. Christians are nice people, but the Muslims cause trouble everywhere in the world. [Hindus] are shooting themselves in the foot [by accommodating Muslims]. The pendulum has to have balance [for Hindus' rights]," he added.

Manni, a fifty-five-year-old computer engineer from Long Island, took a more cultural route to his support of the Hindu right in India. He grew up in a Brahmin family and received his basic engineering education in India. He took his doctorate at UCLA and started his own microchip company, eventually selling it to a major computer hardware firm. Manni stressed his Brahmin heritage, showing me the "sacred thread" he wore around his neck to signify his caste identity. "I sit on the fence on whether there is a God or not. Ethics is more important. My background is more philosophical than religious," he said. To him, Hinduism has always been about tradition and a sense of belonging, but "I don't know if I value tradition more because it's Indian or because it's Hindu." Yet Manni follows most of the Hindu traditions. He is a strict vegetarian, has Hindu shrines in his house, teaches children Hindu prayers and hymns, attends the temple (because of his Brahmin heredity he can and has functioned as a priest in his temple), and even lectures and debates on Hinduism. He stressed that he is doing these activities more because of culture than faith.

In the same way, he supports the Bharatiya Janata Party (BJP) in India "not because it's a Hindu party, but because it's trying to focus on Indian values. I oppose many of its hardline stances. But the Islamic influence in India has to be reduced. I don't believe we can progress if Islam predominates." The connection many interviewees made between Hinduism and scientific advancement was often juxtaposed with statements on the backwardness of Muslims (and, in the American context, conservative Christians). But critics' portrayal of upwardly mobile immigrant professionals as being alienated or rootless and thus susceptible to nationalist and chauvinistic (or fundamentalist) rhetoric is in a way reductionistic and too simple. Peter van der Veer (2005) writes that the idea that professionals working in technology are rootless "misunderstands the imaginary nature of roots. To have roots requires a lot of work for the imagination (dream-work). One element of that dream-work is that pride in one's nation of origin is important in the construction of self-esteem in the place of immigration. It gives a different feeling to admit that one is from a country ravaged by famines and floods than to say with pride that one is from a superior civilization that is also very good in high-tech developments."

It is also unlikely that such attitudes signal wide and deep support for and potential involvement in Hindu nationalism or Hindutva. Prima Kurien (2007) writes that the mass of Hindu devotees around the country are distant from the small group of "ideologues" promoting Hindutva. But she adds that many American Hindus have "internalized" Hindu nationalist ideas, often because of the wide range of resources offered by Hindutva umbrella organizations and websites. The fuzzy nature of Hindutva in the United States is increasingly recognized by scholars. In a study of Hindus in Northern California, Hindutva influence was present in the majority of temples, but it is being "recast." The original political and nationalist intentions of the movement are often rejected by American Hindus who stress Hinduism as a religion and a spiritual system. This ambivalence about politics is found in groups such as the Hindu Students Council—often claimed to be a seedbed of Hindutva in the United States—though nationalist influence is evident in children's educational material presenting the history of India (Sippy 2005). The secularist critique that believing Hindu applied scientists are trying to escape modernity and "true science" by recourse to "tradition," religious nationalism, or fundamentalism also misses the point. As van der Veer notes: "There is no reason at all to expect Hindu engineers and scientists to 'lose their religion' and become secular. Hindu modernity includes an ideological valuation of science and technology. . . . The coherence of a Hindu modernity tied to the sovereignty of India's past and territory is gradually [giving] way to a postmodem bricolage of deterritorialized and dehistorized discourses on family values and cyber-spirituality which is very hard to capture. Contrary to what their opponents think, these movements are not 'outside of modernity'; they are very much part of it and are now moving beyond it" (van der Veer 2005: 288–289). Van der Veer (2014: 191) adds that the "technologies of the self," which embrace spiritual techniques of the body, such as yoga, as well as the idea that work is a form of self-realization, are developed in correspondence with the "soft skills" of the information-based new economies.

Sareeta Amrute (2010) argues that the Hindu IT professional makes use of a multilayered discourse on science, religion, and politics that "reaches down into longstanding traditions of Hindu thought." In studying the discourse of young IT professionals abroad, Amrute writes that they have appropriated the ancient Hindu practice of "appropriateness" or "ritual calibration," holding that religious practice "needs to be carefully tuned away from either secular nationalist or Hindu nationalist ideas and towards a practice that enables ITers to have agency over their own future." The practical, therapeutic, and spiritualizing aspects of Hindu discourse that I have documented do not so much show diluting (under secularization) nor purifying (under fundamentalism) tendencies as much as a way of balancing the demands of the workplace, the home, and the self under global capitalism (Amrute 2010: 542).

CONCLUSION

The Indian Hindu community shows sharp cleavages between middle- and upper-class professionals (mostly doctors, engineers, and computer scientists) and lower-status recent immigrants, such as cab drivers and service industry workers (Lessinger 2001). There are divisions within the professional class. The medical professionals, with their stronger networks of influence in the Indian-American community, have gained access to high levels of Hindu leadership, often serving on the board of directors of temples. The applied science professionals' main avenue of influence is in their religious-scientific discourse dispersed in both formal (in certain temples) and informal (on the Internet) settings. The professional class, with its greater access to travel and business connections, has maintained ties to India that have also exposed the class to transnational movements, such as Hindu revivalism and nationalism.

Van der Veer notes the global nature of the attempt to embrace and "creatively translate science in Hindu civilizational terms" (van der Veer 2005). While Hindu nationalism has clearly political aims in India, the movement's anti-Muslim politics don't make much sense abroad, and in the United States it has been transformed into a global spiritual movement. In the United States, Hindutva's concerns focus more on passing on the faith and traditions to the next generations and maintaining a cultural link between the diaspora and India. While there was some Hindu nationalist sympathy among the interviewees, often expressed by their support of the BJP, it is not clear that Hindu fundamentalism is the same thing as the rationalized Hindu discourse I heard in the interviews. Hindu applied science professionals in the United States may value the spirituality they find in global Hindu nationalism, but place little value on its politics in their new pluralistic surroundings.

Because applied science professionals exert much of their influence outside of the formal temple structure and its rituals and primarily shape the educational and intellectual currents of Hinduism in the United States, such discourse is unlikely to influence the more recent immigrants. But as Indian Hindus seek to assimilate they are more likely to encounter rationalized religious discourse, such as in suburban temples, the Hindu media, and Hindu student groups at universities. This is especially true because the Indian Hindu path to assimilation into American society has largely been through highlighting the religion's rational and scientific outlook and how such a spiritual approach is congruent with modernity. There is no one road to rationalization, especially in a religion as varied and decentralized as Hinduism. It remains to be seen whether the recasting of a mystical and ritual-based religion into more rationalized forms will mean its revitalization or domestication.

Chapter Three

Sikhism, Science, and the Ethic of Prosperity

Just as Sikhism emerged at the crossroads of Muslim and Hindu societies, its relation to science has been shaped by encounters with the rationalistic Islamic worldview and Hindu mysticism. The Sikh religion was founded during the fifteenth century in India's Punjab region by Guru Nanak and continued to develop through ten successive gurus, completing its revelation with its scriptures the *Guru Granth Sahib*. With approximately thirty million adherents, Sikhism is the world's fifth largest religion. Today there are well over five hundred thousand Sikhs in the United States, with the largest and oldest communities existing on the East and West coasts. In a similar way to American Muslims and Hindus, Sikh immigrants, particularly the latest wave since the 1970s, arrived in America as skilled workers, using their technical and business expertise to gain considerable upward mobility.

The Sikh temple I visited occupies an old mansion on a hill overlooking a golf course and beyond that Long Island Sound. As I entered the building, the setting was similarly opulent, though in an Eastern style, with a large crystal chandelier illuminating an oriental carpet and a portrait of Guru Nanak. Before being allowed into the temple proper, I was advised to remove my shoes and then an usher wrapped a large scarf around my head to serve as a makeshift turban.

In entering the temple, or gudwara, I found the assembly divided by gender and sitting on the floor before an elderly man with a long beard bearing a striking resemblance to Guru Nanak and indeed serving as a symbolic stand-in for the founder. He was flanked by a semi-circle of assistants and musicians who led the congregation in readings, chants, and Punjabi singing. The sermon was also delivered in Punjabi, but translations were provided by young people at its conclusion. One of its themes came from a reading of the Sikh holy book, the Guru Granth, about how one should not be "rooted in wealth but in the love of God."

After the service I was introduced to a distinguished-looking man who was an "engineer by profession," but now a real estate investor. He reached behind a counter and quickly produced three stylishly published books he had authored that compared Sikh teachings with those of the other world religions. Before I could ask him any questions, we were all summoned down to the temple's basement for the langar—the free communal meal traditionally served after worship. The congregants sat cross-legged on the floor in three or four rows across the social hall while servers came by with huge pots ladling out servings of rice, roti, and other specialties of the Punjab.

While our plates were being filled, the engineer-turned-investor inquired further about my research. He nodded his head appreciatively as I mentioned how I had heard Sikhs were prominent in the IT and engineering fields. "I don't mean to disparage other religious bodies, but science is right in our text . . . Creation is portrayed in scientific terms, that it came out of a vacuum or the big bang."

As I was getting ready to leave after the meal, I met a professor of anatomy at a prominent university in New York who viewed the large number of Sikh science professionals as an old story. He said that the first generation of Sikh professionals in the United States were engineers, but they are now being followed by lawyers, investors, and academics. He added that the interesting thing was how today a Sikh trained in engineering might start off in that field but over time switch to these newer professions.

In fact, I met several former Sikh engineers during my research who had made the transition to working in finance. Even those still working in these applied science fields were more likely to have moved into high management or started their own companies than the Hindus and Muslims I interviewed. American Sikh professionals seem to be poised at the intersection of American science and capitalism. The corollary Robert Merton drew between the Protestant ethic of capitalism and the Protestant ethic of science, or economic rationalization and scientific rationalization, seems particularly relevant in the case of the Sikhs. Both Sikhs and Protestants emphasize the importance of discipline and on living their faith in society rather than seeking an ascetic escape from the world.

While both belief systems do not hold to holy mediators or institutions of salvation that stand between the believer and the holy text, for the Sikhs the Guru Granth is a living manifestation of the ten Gurus and a terminal point "of a line of belief handed down and deposited in a canon that constitutes the source of spirituality even today" (Pace 2006). Rather than being merely an inspired text as in Protestant Christianity, the Guru Granth functions as an "authoritative, institutionalized religious memory worshipped by the community." This more mystical orientation of Sikhism can be traced to its origins, where Guru Nanak is venerated as the bearer of charisma and of the "extraordinary Word," writes Pace. The Calvinist doctrine of predestination and the corresponding concept of vocation to demonstrate membership in the elect church are alien concepts in Sikhism; as we will see throughout this chapter, Sikh beliefs and practices create a distinctive type of rationality, in both science and economic life, that is somewhat different from that of the Hindus and Muslims, as well as from the Protestant ethic.

THE LIMINAL IDENTITY OF SIKHS

Harpreet, a thirty-five-year-old computer programmer for a large bank, re-counted, still in a tone of disbelief, how he was standing outside his building in lower Manhattan when he saw the Twin Towers attacked and then crumble to the ground in an incendiary cloud of smoke on September 11. He hurried near to the site and said he felt obligated to help in the rescue effort, but were expressly warned away by the police. Harpreet was told that it would be doubly dangerous for him, since bystanders seeing his turban might believe he was one of the terrorists. The unity and sense of purpose of Sikhs were dramatically heightened after the attacks of September 11. Shortly after the attacks a Sikh man in Arizona was murdered by someone mistaking him for a Muslim (with similar incidents occurring up to the time of this writing in 2014). Almost every interviewee had become more outspoken about their faith and its teachings and practices in the aftermath of September 11, hoping to particularly disassociate Sikhism from Islam. Several who had never spok-en about Sikhism were invited (or got themselves invited) by fire depart-ments, schools, and churches to make presentations on the distinctive teach-ings of Sikhism and the wearing of the 5 Ks, consisting of uncut hair (the turban), a comb, a steel wrist guard, a small sword, and short breeches. Most of the professionals had also engaged in more one-on-one conversations with co-workers about their faith since September 11. Thus the confrontation with Islam (in its most extreme form) has once again challenged Sikhs as they have become both more concerned with their own image in society and with articulating the tenets of their faith to outsiders (Mann 2006). This intensified articulation of the faith has been taken up mainly by educated professionals, making their religious discourse particularly prominent in the representation of Sikhism in American society.

The comparisons between Sikhism and Protestantism only carry one so far in understanding this relatively young religion. Sikhism has always had a liminal identity, existing somewhere between Hinduism and Islam, both in the popular imagination and in the actual history of the religion. Up until the late ninteenth century, Sikhism consisted of a series of local communities and traditions interrelated with Muslim and Hindu traditions. The boundaries between these religions were not firmly set in place, and it was not uncommon that those who followed Sikh gurus might also make a pilgrimage to the shrine of a Muslim saint or visit the Ganges for healing. Harjot Oberoi (1994) writes that in the nineteenth century the Sikh faith had a pluralist framework that allowed its adherents to belong to several different traditions and gurus. Many of these Sikhs shaved their heads and smoked tobacco, while others were not diligent about maintaining the five external symbols of the religion. In the absence of a centralized religious authority, a diversity of religious beliefs, rituals, and lifestyles were freely acknowledged.

It was not until the late ninteenth century that a growing movement of Sikhs sought to purge their faith of such pluralism and particularly what were felt to be Hindu influences. In place of such pluralism, the influential Khalsa tradition of Sikhs became the dominant authority, elevating the Guru Granth and the gudwara (or temple) as its main sacred element. It was in this complex interplay of Khalsa influence and the role of colonialists and other religions in constructing (and classifying) a tri-faith India—Hindu, Muslim and Sikh—that Sikhism began to develop an identity for itself over and against Hinduism and Islam.

Sikhs arrived fairly early as immigrants to the United States, arriving in the early 1900s mostly as farm workers in California after escaping from the anti-Oriental riots in Canada in 1907. It was not until the post-1965 period, after immigration laws were relaxed to allow non-European immigration, that a large wave of Sikh professionals and students came directly from the Punjab and the cities of India to the United States, following patterns similar to Hindu immigrants. The new immigrants established much of the religious infrastructure of Sikhism in the United States, founding gudwaras and other religious and cultural associations. Until fairly recently, the establishment of Sikh identity and a public face for the religion in the United States has been complicated and interrupted by conflicts in India, most vividly illustrated by the Indian army's occupation of the most sacred shrine at Amritsar, which Sikhs refer to as their Vatican, in 1984, as well as by internal political conflicts in gudwaras (Williams 1998; Mann 2006) .

MORE RELIGIOUS THAN SPIRITUAL?

Prandeep was only twenty-five years old, but with his impressive turban, long beard, and sleek business suit, he looked much older—and taller. The effect was intentional; the wearing of the 5 Ks signifies maturity and discipline in the Sikh faith. A military ethos has pervaded the religion ever since Sikhs lived under Mogul rule early in their formation and then fought for their own homeland in the early twentieth century. Although none of the interviewees had actually served in the military, they extolled the discipline of the soldier and applied such values to their professional lives. Indeed, "discipline" was often cited as the most important way their faith influences their work.

Prandeep, an IT consultant with a telecommunications firm in New York, emigrated from New Delhi, India, in 2001 to attend college. He was not different from his young Muslim and Hindu counterparts in coming to the realization that his beliefs were in the minority in the United States and that it would take more intentionality and effort to maintain his faith. Prandeep came from a devout family and was very much involved in Sikh life in New Delhi, but he has since come to a more critical view of Sikhism in India. "I'm more of an American Sikh than an Indian Sikh. In India the Sikh religion is absorbing things from other religions, like Hinduism. You don't need to do that. You have to question things. I have cousins and other family [in India] not believing in the religion but they follow it. Here, when people stay Sikh, they know what they are doing." Yet he eventually wants to return to India, even if it may be difficult, largely because of the greater Sikh presence there. He said he maintains his faith because "Sikhism is a very sacrilegious religion—we believe everybody is good. We accept everyone. In the Guru Granth, we even have writings from those of other religions. That's very important in today's society. But we also believe in standing up for ourselves and others. It's a very practical religion—there's spirituality but also warfare." Prandeep said that his faith's main relationship with his work is the way that "Sikhism makes us inquisitive about things. We believe in doing things; it's progressive. I use the same attitude in work. If I believe in something, I'll go for it. I won't be scared. It gives you more confidence."

It was this combination of the ethical and the practical aspects of Sikhism that appealed to the Sikh professionals I interviewed. While Sikhism has a strong mystical component, it was the ethical teachings, particularly as taught by founder Guru Nanak written in the Guru Granth involving equality and social justice, that were the most often cited. As we saw in the last chapter, the popular mantra, "I'm spiritual but not religious," was repeated most often by Hindus. Even when Sikhs used similar terminology, they more often meant that they were less fond of the institutional ("religious") aspects of Sikhism than its more interpersonal and ethical ("spiritual") teachings. Ethical behavior and social justice (expressed in a concern for equality, honesty, not cheating, disloyalty, even being on time to work) was derived less from spiritual and mystical experiences than from mental and even physical discipline. For one thing, not cutting one's hair and wearing the turban and other 5 Ks has a disciplining function in itself. As Randhir, a thirty-six-year-old IT networking and hardware specialist, said: "As a Sikh, you stand out; you [have to] be better behaved and serve as a good example. You're always in the spotlight because of your appearance."

The wearing of the turban served as a self-reminder of the Sikh's duties; it externally and internally reinforces the obligation not to let one's "people" down or dishonor the community or the religion. The Sikh professionals' stress on discipline and "doing one's duty" on the job was strongly tied to the idea that they are "marked out" in society by their dress (the "uniform of Sikhs," as one interviewee said) and feel obliged to live up to their calling. The principle of tolerance toward others may have also been stressed in the interviews because Sikhs are making an effort in the post-9/11 environment to disassociate themselves from Muslims and the stereotypes of religious intolerance surrounding them. Nevertheless, the other disciplines of the faith, daily prayers, scripture reading, meditation, attendance at the gudwara, as well as the general solidarity of the religious community, were seen as encouraging altruistic behavior that extended beyond the basics of hard work and decency on the job.

Ravindra, a thirty-one-year-old civil engineer working in the Long Island firm his father started, described himself as "devout, though not necessarily orthodox." He was one of the few American-born interviewees, but in some ways he was more of a traditionalist than some of the more recently arrived professionals. When I asked him about problems he sees in American Sikhism, he pointed to a nearby gudwara that had broken with tradition by allowing some of its non-elderly members to sit on chairs during the worship service rather than everyone sitting on the floor (usually only the elderly are allowed to sit in chairs in most gudwaras). Such a change (which has led to conflicts and even violence in other Sikh communities in the United States and Canada) violates the Sikh traditional teaching of equality, he said. Ravindra said he has become increasingly "staunch" in his observance of the faith since his college days, citing his abstinence from alcohol. He said the "discipline" of the faith "saved" him from doing things in the past he might regret now. He has recently learned to read and write Gurmukhi, the sacred language in which the Guru Granth was written.

In discussing how his faith has influenced his work, Ravindra pointed to his father as the model of a Sikh engineer and businessman. "I take a lot from my father; the way he treats people equally. . . . He [views the] company like his extended family. That's a direct relation to how his religion affects his work. He has the best benefits package around that really tries to help people." Ravindra recounted how one employee who was frequently ill and missing work was considered being dropped by the health plan and how his father intervened to help her retain her health benefits.

AMERICAN SIKH IDENTITY

The pattern of becoming "more Sikh" upon immigrating to the United States while losing the thick sense of religious community in India was similar to the Muslim and Hindu cases. Sustaining Sikh identity became an active project, necessitating new structures and practices that would manage the risk of the immigrant losing his or her own faith, not to mention that of their children. The interviewees saw some definite losses in this process. When I was invited out for a beer at a Long Island bar by three Sikh IT professionals in their thirties, I wasn't sure if this was unusual or not. Alcohol is not strictly prohibited for all Sikhs, only for those who have been baptized and have embraced the 5 Ks. My three fellow beer drinkers admitted that baptism is far more routine in India; in the United States, the ceremony can be held off indefinitely until a Sikh feels prepared and committed, with many never undergoing it. All three of these Sikhs were highly involved in their gudwaras, but were "working toward" their baptisms. They reported a high level of communal life and devotion, including home observance, such as reciting prayers and readings from the Guru Granth, along with the realization that maintaining orthodox Sikhism was not always possible.

As mentioned in the last section, in the absence of full commitment to orthodox Sikhism, not cutting one's hair and wearing the turban often became the marker of Sikh identity in the United States. As Prandeep said, "It shows you have discipline. If you cut your hair you become an outcast. It's an identity thing." But the decision to refrain from cutting one's hair was not so much a sign of dramatic recommitment to the faith as much as a religious tradition passed down within families. Any greater individual religious commitment usually developed some time after or independently of wearing the turban and the other 5 Ks.

Jasswinder, a fifty-six-year-old founder and CEO of an IT consulting firm in New York, was the only male interviewee who cut his hair. He grew up in a strict Punjabi Sikh home, refraining from eating meat and drinking alcohol. His family moved to England in his teen years, and to avoid ostracism he started cutting his hair. Today he has mixed feelings about going against religious tradition. But he maintains that a "good person is clean inside-out, not outside-in. You can look like a saint [but] you have to judge people by their actions, not by what they say or [their appearance]." The same goes for baptism—"It doesn't make you a better person. There are three simple rules: Honest living, share earnings with others, and remember God." Jasswinder, who is also active in his gudwara, added that following the 5 Ks is the way to get an "A grade in Sikhism. But still, I can get a B+ without that."

This tendency to adapt religious observance and rules to one's own situation and needs was evident among the Muslim and Hindu professionals, but was most pronounced among the Sikhs. But such adaptability was often accompanied by a high level of group solidarity, evident not only in gudwara involvement but also in socializing among and even working with other Sikhs. Gudwara attendance was not always an accurate indicator of involvement in the Sikh community. For instance, Jasdal, a forty-year-old IT application developer for a major New York bank, has varied his gudwara attendance over his lifetime. Like the other Sikhs interviewed, he grew up in a devout home and then fell away only to become more involved and religious in his senior year at an American college. But with the added responsibilities of marriage and children, he attends the gudwara less. Yet he has started a home study group to discuss scriptures that meets every two weeks, and he is strongly involved with United Sikhs, a human rights group. About his relatively relaxed religious practice, Jasdal said that Sikhism was best encapsulated in his own adage: "Live life, meditate, and feel good."

The high level of group solidarity, even if not on the same level as found in predominantly Sikh communities in India, was seen as both a help and hindrance to maintaining religious life. Institutional involvement inevitably brings conflict and disagreement, but there was even a move to disassociate the outer- from the inner-kernels of the faith. As with the Muslims and the Hindus, there was a marked tendency of the Sikhs to go outside of official channels (i.e., the Granthi or clergy) when they had questions or dilemmas about the faith. Unsurprisingly, firsthand study of the Guru Granth was the preferred route that most interviewees took to answering their own questions. But there was also a good deal of reliance upon family members, especially parents and grandparents, as informal sources of authority.

The case of Sarvjit, a recently retired civil engineer in Westchester, illustrates the conflict between the institution and personal faith. He grew up in a traditional Sikh home in the Punjab and was eight years old when the region was divided between India and newly formed Pakistan, with his village falling within the boundaries of the latter country. In the late 1960s he came to the United States for graduate studies in engineering at Duke University. As with the other Sikh professionals, he became more personally committed to Sikhism the longer he stayed in the United States. He has taught and written about the faith in Sikh publications. When asked about what sources he turns to for direction in his faith, Sarvjit responded that he makes up his own mind through his own reading. "I'm blessed that I have enough intellect [to decide such matters]. I'm dead-set against the clergy. I don't give two hoots what they think about religion. The [clergy or Granti] are just professionals. They may know a lot but they compromise a lot, too. I have no respect for people actively involved in the religion; they become politicians. [The leadership] has nothing to do with Sikhism; it's pure politics." Yet Sarvjit himself said that both ritual and such practices as following the 5 Ks were important because they provided a framework of discipline for the devout Sikh. "Religion comes in a package that [includes] ritual. If it follows spirituality, it doesn't matter what ritual it is."

The opposition to the "politics" that take place in gudwaras was more strongly voiced by Parkash, a seventy-five-year-old professor of applied mathematics in New York. He said he was once very active in the gudwara but now attends only occasionally because of the politics he encounters there. "I love politics anywhere else, but not the gudwara; I listen to the music and then I go; I don't even socialize [there]."

Because ritual is downgraded and the mediating role of clergy and holy men between the Sikh and God is condemned while serving God through good deeds and holy living are stressed in the Sikh tradition, it is no surprise that there is a strong tendency to disassociate the truth of the religion from its organizational, ritual, and sometimes even dogmatic dimensions. We saw this tendency even among the Hindu professionals—though they more often tended to categorize their beliefs into pillars—but it is a far easier task in Sikhism, especially among professionals trained to think things out for themselves. Both the ritualism of Hinduism and the "dogmatism" of Islam, particularly post-9/11, were points of contrast when the Sikhs spoke of the "this-worldly," practical, and tolerant nature of their faith.

Early in our interview, Parminder, a retired mechanical engineer, declared that the clergy are "my least favorite kind of Sikh." The way in which these Sikh professionals often made the dichotomy between authentic religion and official Sikhism was clarified when I asked Parminder about why he remains a practicing Sikh. "It's the utter simplicity of it. Guru Nanak was a revolutionary visionary who wanted to bring Hindus and Muslims together. He understood that dogma divided. He went to both mosques and [Hindu] temples. He did not promote conversions and [he] preached gender equality. He asked how could women be inferior when they've given birth to kings? There was not a formal priestly class. He said truth is wonderful, but truthful living is higher still. [The religion] is more practical than dogmatic."

The principles of practical living over doctrine, equality over hierarchy, respect for and tolerance toward other religions, and social justice were cited as the most appealing aspects of Sikhism by the interviewees. That these principles were seen as "modern," "scientific," and American made them even more attractive. Several noted the similarities between the principles of the U.S. Constitution and the Sikh religion, particularly the focus on equal rights for everyone. Armeet, a forty-six-year-old sales executive for an IT firm on Long Island, said that the part of Sikhism that is most compelling is its call for "justice, equality, and human rights. It's very straightforward and like the American approach—civil rights, what's in the Bill of Rights, and to defend that." In fact, the Sikh support for a homeland in Khalistan, which is often considered an earmark of Sikh fundamentalism, was little in evidence among the interviewees. Most kept in contact with India, usually through visits to relatives and to prominent temples in the Sikh holy city Armistar, as well as through contributing to and volunteering for international Sikh causes (through a group such as United Sikhs, for example). Support for a Sikh homeland was based more on respect for the general (and American) principle of self-determination rather than religious teaching. Most discounted Sikh nationalism as a distraction from the ideals of social justice and the importance of unity rather than division between people. The appreciation for American pluralism in strengthening their own personal faith made most of them wary of returning to or creating a totally Sikh society. For Sarvjit, the retired engineer, the cause of a Sikh homeland is "pure politics; it has nothing to do with Sikhism."

Although Sikh "fundamentalism" is a contested and controversial term, it is often used to denote allegiance to Khalistan as the Sikh homeland, as well as the belief in the inerrancy of the Sikh sacred texts (although, as noted earlier, the meaning of inspiration of the Guru Granth is quite different than that found in Christian or Islamic fundamentalism) (McLeod 2001). Whether fundamentalist or not, Ranjit, a thirty-three-year-old engineer with an electronics firm in New Jersey, was clearly more conservative (with, as we will see in the next section, quite different views of science and religion) than the other Sikh interviewees. He was brought up in a strict religious home in Bombay. But it was only after arriving in the U.S. in 2000 that he applied such strictness to his own religious practice. This greater discipline, which includes rising very early for prayers and scripture study and going to the gudwara every morning, is the main way that he said his faith has grown since coming to the United States.

Ranjit said his faith has developed "inner" and "outer" dimensions. The outer dimension is "more about how to improve behavior; how to behave with other humans and other creatures." Like the others, he said he finds the "tolerance, fighting against injustice, honest living, and loyalty" the most appealing features of Sikhism. Ranjit added that he has also become more "enlightened" about the inner dimensions of Sikhism, particularly in understanding the Guru Granth. The meaning of the text becomes clear through spiritual enlightenment without the help of scholars who could interpret it. In contrast, most of the other Sikh professionals saw the Guru Granth as open to various interpretations. Unlike the others, Ranjit stressed a distinctly hierarchical view of religious authority. Each gudwara is not independent but under the authority of the main temple in Amritsar in the Punjab. "It is the highest authority, like the Vatican or the White House, and settles issues [in Sikhism]," he said (while most interviewees accepted the authority of Amritsar, they were more likely to stress local solutions to religious controversies). In a similar way, the right to a Sikh homeland is an important part of Ranjit's faith. While he doesn't believe he will see Sikhs settled in a homeland in his lifetime, Ranjit keeps this possibility "in his heart." Part of the appeal of

Khalistan is that it will be separate from India, which he does not believe is a real democracy, and will be run on Sikh principles; "95 percent of Sikh laws are like U.S. laws," he added. Thus, even the most orthodox Sikh interviewee turned to the United States as a model and inspiration for his dream of a religious homeland.

SIKH SCIENCE

The Sikh professionals were very similar to their Muslim and Hindu counterparts professionals in claiming, if not a distinct science dictated by their religion, at least a religion most advanced in terms of promoting and accommodating scientific progress. As with the Muslims and Hindus, many of the Sikhs pointed to their sacred text as foreshadowing scientific advancements. Like the Hindus and unlike the Muslims, the Sikhs did not so much cite the Guru Granth for its scientific accuracy as a way to prove the infallibility and divine inspiration of the text. Rather, the text was viewed as documenting how individuals who receive "enlightenment" are on par with scientists in their knowledge of the natural world. Thus a popularly written book on Sikh basic beliefs states that "modern science, now, has concluded with authority the indestructibility of mass or matter. But ancient GURUS, SEERS and PROPHETS could long ago declare this TRUTH, with assertive authority, gained intuitively. Soul is consciousness. Without the soul, the body is only a skeleton. After death, the subtle body rises out of the gross body" (Singh 1998: 79). Other treatments of Sikhism and science stress the scientific nature of the religion over other faiths. One book concludes that "Sikhism walks hand in hand with modem scientific and technological theories. . . . The general instruction of Sikhism is to rationalize every opinion before accepting it and to continuously engage in research" (Sidhu 2003: 175; for another example of Sikh use of science, see Sikhism FAQs 2007). But other treatments of science by Sikhs are less sure of an easy fit with religion. An anthology (2012) bringing together Sikh scientists on the question of the harmony between science and Sikhism, ranged from defenses of Stephen Jay Gould's idea of the "non-overlapping magisterias" of faith and science to expositions of the scriptures to prove their scientific basis. The former view is clearly held by contributor I. J. Singh as he questions those who espouse the idea that Sikhism is a "scientific religion," and argues that scientific theories "are never dogmatically held, only tentatively embraced; they are modified, even jettisoned, if newer data so warrant. . . . Religious truths need to be internally consistent, logical, and not at conflict with reality as it continues to be unfolded to us by time and technology. But they are not testable, nor are they meant to be incomplete—to be modified or abandoned as nature unfolds its reality before us" (Singh 2012: 151–152).

Several of those I interviewed tended toward the embrace of a scientific religion. The Sikh engineer-turned-investor we met at the beginning of this chapter spoke about how the big bang theory of the earth's origin is already found in the Guru Granth. However figurative and allegorical it may be, the language of the texts do address creation in a way that invited scientific speculation from the interviewees. The Guru Granth refers to the "Primal Void" from which the "earth and the Ethers were created" (Guru Granth 1037, cited by Singh 1998: 26). This "void" is often translated as a "vacuum" and then portrayed in a scientific manner relating to the big bang theory. Several of the interviewees cited many other teachings and accounts from the Guru Granth that allegedly had scientific significance. The reference to millions of universes in the text was related to the growing number of planets discovered. Einstein's theory that energy can't be created or destroyed but only transformed was first laid out when Sikh gurus taught that humanity is all part of a cycle. Another IT professional mentioned that the development of nanotechnology, or micro-devices, was foreshadowed in the Guru Granth.

The highly orthodox Ranjit was the most enthusiastic about such Sikh-science convergences. He said the Guru Granth is a "book of life and knowledge, not just a book of religion." Whereas most of the other professionals accepted a theory of evolution without many problems, Ranjit said he "doesn't believe it. The [Guru Granth] teaches that God created humans directly in just a fraction of a second." Ranjit was also unique in the way he incorporated mystical, even esoteric, concepts into his views of science. He believes that Sikhs who have reached an "inner enlightenment" can, if not in this life then in later reincarnations, see how the universe was created and actually experience the "black hole," or the void from which creation emerged. Disciplined living and meditation made such feats possible. Once the "mind [reaches] enough enlightenment," the Sikh can leave his body and explore alternate universes. Returning to a more empirical approach, Ranjit added that recent scientific research has verified such a phenomenon.

Most of the interviewees took a far different position than Ranjit in relating science to religion. Even if some might agree that Sikh gurus and the Guru Granth had made valid scientific observations, they seemed more interested in showing how Sikhism was in line with modem scientific thought than in claiming Sikh roots and preeminence in science. In such a view, Sikhism is the "most scientific" and "most modern" religion because it conforms to the demands and rubrics of modem science. In one way, this could be done by default, with the belief that Sikhism does not have much to do with or is removed from science. Randhir, the thirty-six-year-old IT hardware specialist, said that he could not recall any references to science in all the sermons he had heard at his gudwara or in the Guru Granth itself. "There's no science in it. It's all about how to act and behave and how to improve yourself." Some believed that the lack of explicit references to science in Sikhism was because of the lack of conflict and controversy over this issue as compared to other religions. The civil engineer, Ravindra, said, "It's a very modern and scientifically based religion. It's five hundred thirty years old. The big bang, evolution; there's no conflict [over these]. Our basic philosophy is that science is okay. In the Guru Granth, I never witnessed anything remotely like scientific theory, just the general philosophy of how to live life." Jasdal, the forty-year-old programmer for a bank, said that he is "not one who explains religion through science. I don't feel we have to judge the holy book with a scientific yardstick. I take it for granted that the Guru Granth is ahead of science [though] we don't have to use it [that way]."

Also common was the recasting, if not the transformation, of Sikh beliefs into a more scientific mold. This tendency was very clear in the account of twenty-five-year-old IT executive Prandeep. In explaining the doctrine of reincarnation, he said it could not be proven scientifically, and he has had trouble believing in it himself. "My own personal belief is that every religion has its own form of scaring people into good behavior. It's psychological, [and] when you grow up you see it as a scare tactic. It has a purpose, but scientifically, I don't believe in it. But I wouldn't [say] that to . . . those younger in the faith."

Ravindra said that the accounts of miraculous healings in the Guru Granth and popular Sikh legends could likewise be explained by unrecognized medical cures that were mistaken for the supernatural. For instance, a guru in scriptures is reported to have healed a village of small pox. "But they were just stories passed down [from one generation to another]; it was probably just medicine," he added. In a religion that lacks a central teaching authority, there were sharp divisions among the Sikhs about the nature of miracles. Prandeep said he believes the "supernatural is also the natural," meaning that supposedly supernatural events can be explained in naturalistic terms. But most of the interviewees were uneasy in ceding too much ground to a rigid naturalism that excluded divine intervention.

This way of portraying themselves as modern, scientific professionals holding to an equally modern faith while maintaining faith in an active, interventionist God is nicely illustrated in the remark of the retired civil engineer, Sarvjit, which I cited in part in the introduction: "You'll see that I look at religion from the perspective of my profession and education," he said. "Everybody looks at religion from [the perspective of] their own professions . . . I'm an engineer, so things should add up. If it doesn't, then something is wrong. In engineering, [something] is irrelevant if it doesn't happen in the real world. In engineering, I don't care about electricity unless it makes the light bulb [work]. The same with religion. It doesn't mean a thing if it doesn't give you satisfaction." As with the Muslim and Hindu professionals I interviewed, the Sikhs often drew a distinction between the theoretical and applied sciences, arguing that the latter was more concerned with the "real world" and actual results rather than with speculation and generalized explanation. Sarvjit criticized such scientific methods as prediction and extrapolation since they rely on "imagination," meaning that they are based on future events and data which don't exist and "don't affect life." In this way, he also criticized theories of evolution since they are conjectures and reconstructions of developments and events from the distant past. In this view, science is more partial and incomplete than scientists are willing to admit. "Whenever you get answers to questions, you always get more questions. You never get there, but you should always keep trying [to find the answers]," he said. This is where religion enters the picture, since the endless and incomplete nature of science "does not teach ethics. But it says to be humble. Most of religious philosophy explains the part [of reality] science can't explain."

For most of the Sikh interviewees, the incomplete nature of science and the practical and "real world" basis of applied science created a scenario where the spheres of religion and science rarely clashed and were often viewed as complementary. If a particular scientific development conflicted with a religious teaching, the latter could be downplayed as irrelevant or reinterpreted as more symbolic than literal. In a similar way, a troublesome scientific finding could be viewed as partial and thus misleading, something that could be set right by new data in the future. These strategic views allowed for the possibility of divine intervention in mundane affairs, even if there was considerable disagreement about the nature of miracles among the Sikh professionals. For Sarvjit, "God works within the [natural] system. Miracles don't happen." But others maintained that supernatural occurrences, such as healings, suspended scientific laws and could be valid. Harpreet, the IT executive working for a New York bank and among the more orthodox of the Sikhs, believed that through meditation one could control one's world, though Sikhism calls the believer to renounce such powers. "This is what Guru [Nanak] did. He said the biggest miracle was to share your bread with someone."

Jasswinder, the founder and CEO of an IT firm on Long Island, said that while Sikhism disapproves of demonstrating miraculous powers in order to prove God's existence, he is convinced that some things are still "unexplained. There is something out there. I don't have a clear knowledge of what it is. I can't convince others but I can I try to convince myself." He also drew on his profession in explaining his approach to religious and scientific concepts he can't prove. "I'm an engineer. Logically speaking, some things are out of my control and I leave it there and don't worry about it. If I haven't done my own homework, I can't say something doesn't exist." In this way, Jasswinder sought to cast doubt on both religious and scientific certainty.

TECHNOLOGY AND THE WILL OF GOD

There was little doubt or uncertainty when it came to the value and importance of technology among the Sikh professionals. The professionals in Islam and Hinduism showed a high level of admiration and support of technology along with some trepidation about its abuses. But the Sikhs' belief in technology was different in kind as well as degree from the others. Unqualified support may be the wrong term, since these interviewees did not necessarily oppose attempts to curb such progress when it proved harmful. The case of Armeet, the forty-six-year-old woman sales executive for a Long Island IT firm, may help illustrate such attitudes. She grew up in a traditional Sikh family in New Jersey. While she has been active in her gudwara, running its education program, she has also dissented from Sikh orthodoxy. She has cut her hair and does not carry the dagger, another one of the 5 Ks. The most appealing aspect of Sikhism for her is that the religion is "very flexible, very fair . . . treating men and women equally. Any inequality in it is manmade. It's very simple—there are no rituals and special prayers. It teaches mutual respect and that good will happen if you do this."

Armeet sees her faith as instrumental in her success. "Because the religion teaches us to be fair, honest, and good people, we carry that into the business world. The payback is immense. The religious difference [of being a Sikh] has been an asset. The interest that others have [in Sikhism] creates a bond and is instrumental in me being a success. Our talk about religions leads to deeper conversations; it's not all about business." The benefits of the faith also blend the business and personal aspects. "Because my job is closing [sales] for the company, you can only take transactions so far. It's out of your hands. It's destiny. No matter what I do, [sometimes] it's not going to happen."

The same acceptance of destiny was on display in Armeet's view of technology and the relation between science and religion. On the latter question, she answered that she saw some conflict between the two spheres, but her sympathies were not with the religious side. "I'm glad from the science standpoint that they don't let religion stand in their way. I'm glad the scientific community doesn't let their [own] beliefs stop them [in their work]." Asked about the advance of biotechnology and associated issues, ranging from abortion to stem cell research and cloning, Armeet replied, "I am in favor of it, the abortion act and the [other] technology being applied. . . . Because of technology, like the Web, we have so much. . . . [It's] destiny, and I generally support such measures." Although Armeet's view on abortion was not shared by all the professionals, her reference to technology being "destiny" was echoed throughout my interviews. Harpreet, the New York computer programmer, said that technology on the whole is "beneficial," and that "stem cell research is good if used positively. Everything that happens is the will of God. The problems and solutions [of technology] are a manifestation of the will of God." Even the highly orthodox Ranjit said he supports such measures as cloning and stem cell research. "If it's going to happen, it's the will of God. That [means] it's a reality already. If [the development] is too much, God can destroy the planet."

Sarvjit worked in nuclear power before public opposition closed his plant, forcing him into early retirement. To him, it was fear mongering that caused the closure. "Fear is our worse enemy. They [didn't] say we built anything unsafe. The fear was unnecessary and stupid. To say there's a problem is not to do anything to solve it. We do the best we can and keep on moving." Sarvjit also supports stem cell research and cloning, even though some say that such technology is playing God. "This is what God wanted," he added. "Anything that's going to happen emerges or God could stop it. Nothing comes without a price. Happiness will not come with technology. But to refuse to accept technology is just as bad."

As suggested in the case of Sarvjit, such confidence in technology can stem from these professionals' work in this area (and the success that Sikhs have achieved through such work), but that does not explain the connection often made between the will of God and technological progress. Even for the most non-dogmatic Sikh, the belief in "God's order" has come to mean that God controls the good and bad things that happen. As Jasdal, the forty-year-old IT professional, said, "If something happens, then God willed it. The Sikh tries to live in God's good order." It should be stressed that the Sikh treatment of technology, particularly biotechnology, is not all of the rosy hue that was evident in my interviews. But it may say something that one of the strongest Sikh denunciations of biotechnology, including cloning and genetic modification of plants, issues from a philosopher in India rather than an applied or theoretical scientist in the United States (Chahal 2012).

THE SIKH ETHIC OF PROSPERITY

As I made my way through the electronic gate and the tree-lined driveway, which seemed more like a long road, toward the palatial estate of Sirdar, an engineer-turned-real-estate-investor, my mind went back to Weber's Protestant ethic. What effect does such wealth have upon the Sikh professionals and their faith? It is the question with which I began this chapter, though it did not appear to have much to do with Sikhs and science. As I noted earlier, however, economic and scientific rationalization uniquely interacts in the case of the Sikhs. They tended to move up to management level, start their own firms, or move out of applied science fields altogether into finance or business more often than the Muslims and Hindus. For Sirdar, there seemed to be little conflict between his faith and the substantial prosperity he has accumulated with his investments. "The Sikh believes in having wealth. It's not something negative. But we shouldn't get lost in the wealth [which is a verse from the Guru Granth]. It's for the purpose of helping others," he said. The prosperity of those still working in the applied sciences was also seen in a similar way to that of technological progress—part of God's will but also open to abuse. Armeet, the IT sales executive, said that "God's been good. . . . Truly, everything I have is because of God. I'd be nothing without him. I'm in the top 1 percent of women in earning. It's a great thing, but I believe the wealth is in contentment and in [my] kids and a close-knit family." Armeet said she has been helped by some Sikhs in achieving success and, in turn, feels she should help other Sikhs in finding work and making other business contacts. It should be noted, however, that while Sikhs have created and benefited from strong transnational business and entrepreneurial networks, the majority of Sikh professionals I interviewed said they achieved their success largely without assistance from fellow believers.

Randhir, the thirty-six-year-old IT professional, said that he has "been blessed" with the prosperity he has accrued from his work. But he was quick to add that he "went into computers for fun, to explore things, not to make money like the kids today." For a minority the connection between their faith and prosperity was indirect or even remote. The civil engineer Ravindra said he has "never made any relation between my [faith] and prosperity—never tied them together. But religion makes me want to work harder, so it [may] all tie in together." For Kahan, a twenty-nine-year-old chemist at a pharmaceutical company, it makes sense that any religion would contribute to a work ethic, and thus financial success, but he finds it ironic that prosperity is associated with Sikhism. "We were the poorer castes"—one of the reasons the call for radical equality resonated so strongly with the followers of Guru Nanak, he said. There was also some fear among interviewees about the dangers too much wealth posed for the spiritual life. This was clear in the case of the strongly orthodox Ranjit. He said that "wealth can be a good reward from God," but too much money easily leads to greed, one of the "five demons" cited in the Guru Granth (along with lust, anger, attachment, and ego). Achieving such prosperity means that "[God] wants you to give extra." In Ranjit's view, the mature and godly Sikh should engage in "simple living and high thinking."

THE SIKH WAY OF RATIONALIZATION

Even if there was also some agreement among the interviewees with ascetic Protestants that prosperity can be a minefield of temptations and dangers to the faith, on the whole, the Sikhs were able to maintain a balance between an inner piety or mysticism with a strong outward dimension (social justice and equality) and worldly and successful lives in applied science and business. The accumulation of wealth among ascetic Protestants was portrayed by Weber and other historians as an unintended consequence of virtuous living as they sought to prove themselves to be among God's elect. For the Sikhs, the accumulation of wealth was quite intentional (as it is for many Protestants today), even if they saw such prosperity as being subject to the mysteries of God's will. The Sikh believer is called both to achieve mystical union with God while at the same time living and working in this world. This would be close to what Weber called "inner-worldly mysticism"; the world is not rejected but is the "sphere in which contemplative virtues are practiced and the search for the mystical union with God takes place. Therefore, in everyday life and practical work, the inner-worldly mystic lives in the world, respecting the internal autonomy of the various spheres of life, without allowing this recognition to turn itself into an internal conflict between "faith and work," according to Enzo Pace (2005: 2–3).

The risk that defines Weber's Calvinist Protestants in living out their vocation in line with God's commands while being uncertain of their own salvations is foreign to Sikhs who do not have a concept of predestination. It is the more positive concept of "work as worship," which Pace defines as attaining spiritual elevation by "giving your best in the worldly sphere." The Sikh followers learn to "discipline their lives by devoting themselves to the achievement of a goal which is both the practice of the virtue of obedience toward the master [found in the sacred text] and economic and social success. . . ." One's righteous actions ("truthful living") and the discipline of following the 5 Ks trumped mysticism, spirituality, and dogmatic correctness in forming the core of Sikh identity among the interviewees. Obedience and disciplining one's actions and thoughts in pursuit of a sacred goal are among the classic ingredients of rationalization.

Sikhism, like Islam, underwent rationalization as it codified its teachings, excluded diverse traditions, and closed the process of revelation with the passing of its last guru. It can be argued that American Sikhism in the post-9/11 era has been "re-rationalized," as its members (especially articulate professionals) have been forced to explain Sikhism to outsiders in understandable terms and differentiate it clearly from Islam. Sikhism, however, also retained its mystical disposition from Hinduism even as it led members to express their mysticism in worldly pursuits. This tension between the inner-mystical and the worldly and rational runs through the accounts of the Sikh professionals we have met. This dynamic forms a particular logic that is congenial to work in applied science and technology. To begin with, the instrumental approach of the Sikhs is evident even in the way they approach their occupations. For all immigrant professionals, a high-paying position with skills easily transferable between societies, including a minimum of required language skills, is a practical career choice. But the relatively high mobility of the Sikhs, whether it be moving to management levels or switching from applied science to more lucrative lines of work, suggests a more instrumental approach to one's occupation. This does not mean that the Sikhs' sole priority is financial or that they are less devoted to their vocations than other immigrant professionals. But the entrepreneurial orientation of Sikh immigrants allows for more flexibility and choice in the occupational market.

The emphasis on practical action and living a religion instead of adhering to a complex doctrinal system fits in well with a profession more concerned with results and practical solutions rather than methodology and speculative theorizing. For several interviewees, the sentiment that religion, however true, is useless unless it leads to "truthful living," seemed to translate into almost a disdain for scientific reasoning removed from practical realities and benefits. More than Islam and Hinduism, the dominant Sikh Kalsa tradition provided a rationalized template to the religion that has proven uniquely adaptable to Western modernity, whether in its scientific or economic dimensions. The shock waves of secularity that have occurred within these spheres have also been buffeted for the Sikhs by strong community ties and networks enhanced by ethnic and language differences from wider society. Within these subcultural parameters, however, considerable freedom of thought, if not practice, is allowed. The more individualistic and "heterodox" Sikhs—increasingly likely to consist of the younger generations—may find the strictures and popular sentiment within their religious communities as confining and unenlightened, yet they, no less than their more orthodox counterparts, laid claim to their Sikh heritage and identity. This common religious identity has been based on following external rules, such as adhering to the 5 Ks, more than correctness of belief. Because these practices have declined among the young, both in the Punjab and in Sikh diasporas, the perpetuation of such an identity is far from assured (Singh 2014). At the same time, these Sikhs looked back to Guru Nanak and his teachings of radical equality among members and the practice of good works (or living out the truth) as the cornerstones of their religion—concepts which also resonate with both conservative and liberal Sikhs. Again, this concern with equality can reinforce traditionalism, as seen in the vigilance about fellow Sikhs sitting on the floor during worship, or broaden out to embrace social justice for those outside the fold. That both tendencies can be present simultaneously for the Sikhs was seen in the case of Ravindra, who works in his father's civil engineering company. He was very critical of gudwaras that have been too quick to accommodate worshippers with chairs. Yet at the same time he held his father up as the model of the Sikh professional for how he ran the company as an extended family, granting generous benefits to everyone.

Nowhere is the dynamic between worldliness and mysticism seen more vividly than in the Sikh professionals' views on technology. In a way, it seems all too simple: The professionals work with technology and thus see it as a benign force that is part of God's will. It can be argued that the overwhelming embrace of technological progress, including biotechnology, among the Sikhs shows a reliance on disenchanting technical expertise at the expense of mystery and the supernatural. It is also the case that the Muslims and Hindus showed a similar if less pronounced support of technology, suggesting that this pattern could be explained by a diffusion of secular values in occupations largely based on technology, or a non-Western (mostly Southeast Asian and Indian) otherworldliness that takes a benign approach to societal affairs and changes. Both of these explanations should not be discounted and will be discussed more in chapter 4.

Yet the Sikh acceptance of technological advances and changes appears to stem more directly from their distinctive belief in the unfolding of God's will and destiny than from societal and work-related pressures to adapt to a technological society. It entails fostering an internal state of resignation to and acceptance of God's will along with a willingness to participate in the divine plan as it manifests itself in the world. Unlike the Calvinist Protestant, there is no attempt to "remake the world" or steer these worldly processes along more "godly" lines. The mystical acceptance of scientific developments—and everyday life itself—as the unfolding of God's will implies that both problems and their solutions are part of such a destiny and doesn't necessarily imply complete passivity on the part of the believer. The protesting and closing of a nuclear power plant can just as easily fit into this divine scheme as its installation and operation. If things turn out badly, the devout Sikh can reason that "it wasn't meant to be"; the believer still has the assurance that he or she accepted God's will and intended to live out the truth. This is somewhat similar to the boiled-down and even "lite" version of Sikhism provided by Jasdal, the computer programmer: "Live life, meditate, and feel good." But the tendency to see science and values as separate spheres that have little interaction can give technology an autonomy that does not yield to moral agency. Such a stance does not mean so much a rationalization of Sikhism as much as a potential weakening of the religion's outward thrust toward social justice.

Chapter Four

A Shared Religion-Science Discourse

Early in my research when I told a sociologist of my intent to study Hindu engineers and IT professionals and their religious faith, he remarked that Hindus, given their ascetic and mystical orientation, would likely make a clear separation between their faith and their "profane" work. But as I found in chapter 2, the interviewees and much of the literature produced by Hindus in general tend to extol a Hindu work ethic and to meld scientific with religious concepts and language. In fact, it has actually been difficult to predict the ways in which applied science professionals make the connection between their faith and their work.

Part of the reason for this unpredictability is that it is not just a question of Muslim, Hindu, and Sikh professionals interacting with applied science; there are broader factors that shape this encounter, such as immigration, education, professional culture, and the "de-traditionalization" of religion. In this chapter I will examine both these broader forces as well as the way in which these professionals' respective religions and traditions shape their discourse. In comparing Muslim, Hindu, and Sikh involvement in applied science, I am especially interested in how these religions provide resources and tools to their adherents as well as in how these traditions shape and channel their discourses and practices in specific directions. In a somewhat different vein, I will argue that science, and applied science in particular, is not a strictly rational and universal enterprise impervious to culture, values, and ethics.

Throughout this chapter I plan to steer a middle course between viewing science and religion as having unchangeable essences and seeing them largely as social constructions that can be redefined and adapted to cultural changes according to the preferences of their practitioners and adherents. I treat religions as systems which imprint "tracks" through which innovations and change travels; the tracks can be traced back to their origins in these traditions as well as, through interactions with other traditions and social forces, point forward in new and sometimes unpredictable directions. Another way of putting this is that the world religions provide the believer with a repertoire of symbols, responses, language, rituals, meanings, and ethics which have their own logic and directions. Martin (2005) argues that the world religions are "not haphazard assemblies of assorted empirical mistakes, or even useful wisdom hidden away in mythic form, but the strictly limited set of alternative logics as delineated by Max Weber." As I will discuss, drawing such limits to religious logic is not necessarily the same thing as espousing essentialism. Repertoires of religious logic, by their very nature, allow for choice and selectivity, and can change or, in Martin's term, "mutate" over time into new forms, or even be penetrated by (or penetrate into) minority or counter-logics (Martin 2002).

THE ROLE OF IMMIGRATION AND GLOBALIZATION

My reference to different religious repertoires should not gloss over the fact that in several important ways, there are not sharp differences between the Muslim, Hindu, and Sikh applied science professionals and how they relate their faith to their work.[1] It is not difficult to find a shared religion-applied science discourse in the different personal accounts I have recorded in the last three chapters. The professionals share an American professional immigrant (and increasingly global) ethos where technical expertise and lingo supersede a common language and culture in achieving upward mobility and assimilation. Although their reliance on global networks and transnationalism in migration and mobility differs—far more in the case of the Hindus and Sikhs compared to that of the Muslims—they experienced common push and pull factors in leaving the traditional societies of their origins to fulfill their professional aspirations. They went to the same graduate schools upon arriving in the United States and followed a common pattern of regaining or strengthening their faith in the process of immigration and assimilation and establishing careers and families.

It should be stressed that it is the American immigration experience rather than the immigration process in itself that significantly contributes to this convergence of professional and religious discourse. A comparison of the situation of religious immigrants in the United States with that of Europe suggests the importance of national context in the interaction of religion with other spheres of knowledge and society. That Muslims make up the largest share of immigrants in most European countries at the same time that Islam itself is perceived by many as a "non-European" religion obviously creates obstacles not only for the acceptance but for the religious identity and self-image of these "newcomers." If a religion is seen as "foreign" and intrinsically alien by a largely secular host society, then immigrants becoming more religious would tend to be discouraged in adopting a new national identity and integrating into the educational and professional strata of society. Since Muslim immigrants have come into European countries from unskilled and working-class backgrounds (far more than in the United States), those attempting to ascend to professional status run the risk of becoming secularized in the process; one can imagine that trying to relate one's faith to professional life in such a context is problematic.

The situation is quite different in the case of the United States, where religious pluralism and a generally more religious climate tend not to pit immigrant devotion to their religions against the drive toward integration and professional advancement. Because United States immigrants hold to a wider range of world religions than in Europe, such pluralism provides a different environment to that of one large minority religion (such as Islam) existing in relationship to a secular establishment. Along with the cultural pressure to be religious like other Americans, immigrants find that religious identities tend to gain salience in the process of immigrant incorporation into the United States. Not only do immigrant religions often take a Protestant "congregational" form on the local level (in marked contrast to their traditional structures in their home countries), but they also gain equal footing with other religions as they are integrated into a denominational market structure under the separation of church and state (Casanova 2007). Under European church—state models, minority religions are given secondary status under the state churches or face restrictions of their public dimensions (i.e., wearing veils or running their own schools). The (admittedly contested) constraints of American church-state separation still allows for associational freedom and public (though non-governmental) expression for immigrant religions, although for groups such as Muslims the process toward such recognition has been strained, especially since 9/11.

Studies of the development of American Islam and Hinduism find that for such immigrants, claiming a religious identity can serve as an attractive alternative to being viewed in primarily racialized categories (Kurien 2007; Leonard 2003). This is especially the case for upwardly mobile professionals who understand that racial discrimination is far more prevalent than religious discrimination in the American workplace. Thus, stressing both a religious identity and scientific proficiency, and attempting to bridge the two spheres, at least in discourse (in arguing for intelligent design, for example), is advantageous in an American and a global context. The presence of these global religions in the United States and of adherents of these faiths who have the means of receiving and sending resources and knowledge (through technology, donations, travel, and transnational networks) around the world contributes to the globalization of American society. On first appearance, the transnational ties of the interviewees seemed modest. But the transnational and global dimensions became more prominent when considering that most of them (particularly the Indians) traveled to their home countries on a fairly regular basis, contacted family and sometimes religious leaders when they had questions about their faith (particularly the Muslims), donated to international religious causes, and were considering eventually returning to their home countries to assist in social betterment or to cultivate their own spirituality. The two values of scientific proficiency (which bypasses national cultures and languages) and a religious faith which crosses national boundaries make the professionals in this study "global citizens," whether they take advantage of their status or not (Levitt 2007).

AUTODIDACTS IN RELIGION AND SCIENCE

These professionals relied on the tools of their trade, such as firsthand inquiry and investigation and valuing practical effectiveness, as they sought to draw closer to their faiths, rather than following the guidance of religious authorities and institutions. The institutional religious involvement of the interviewees varied, but it is not necessary to generalize from such a small sample to observe that their vocational orientation could easily lead to individualized religion. We saw instances of this in all three groups: the Hindu mechanical engineering professor who saw Hinduism more as a scientific philosophy than as a ritual-based community of faith; the Iranian Muslim computer science student who repudiated both his Shi'ite background and Sunni Islam and seemed to create his own cyber-generated faith made up of online inquiry and private reading and interpretation; or Sarvjit, the retired Sikh civil engineer, who scorned the "politics" of his religious leadership and confessed his uneasiness with participating in his gudwara because of his unpopular and contested views.

These professionals' expertise and their ability to "think things out" for themselves was applied to interpreting sacred texts, leading to a selectivity in emphasizing, de-emphasizing or even discarding particular beliefs and practices. Several interviewees made the point that they were orthodox and traditional, but the ways in which they ordered and articulated their system of belief was often individualized. This was seen with the Hindu mechanical engineering professor Krishna, who could only be described as a religious virtuoso, as he fit together mystical and ritual components into a comprehensive whole, even as he integrated his specialization of acoustics into such a system.

The disinterest in and sometimes outright opposition to clergy and professional religious leadership found among the applied scientists may not be a direct result of religious individualism and autodidactism; there has often been conflict between assimilating immigrants and clergy who are usually more recent (and often temporary) arrivals from the sending countries. These professionals may not be as individualistic as they think; as I will discuss later in this chapter, they are shaped by the American religious culture as much as by their professional environment. The lay-clergy culture gap and the lack of educated clergy in the United States in the Muslim, Hindu, and Sikh traditions surely contribute to the sentiment common in both the interviews and the literature that educated laypeople have to take religious matters into their own hands. The autodidacticism I found among the interviewees is more pronounced largely because engineers and IT professionals have the resources and time to devote to religious self-education and improvement (and also the reason why the retirees were the most active and outspoken religious autodidacts among the interviewees, especially among the Hindus who assign spiritual importance to this later stage of life).

In the literature and Internet-based writings produced by these religious autodidacts, as well as in the interviews, one finds a degree of theological creativity and even improvisation. This is most clearly seen in the attempts to harmonize modem science and technology with traditional teachings. For instance, in trying to come to terms with a sharply contested issue such as evolution, one finds a range of novel readings and interpretations of sacred texts, borrowings from other traditions, and imaginative renderings of their own historical traditions. Ahmed, the Muslim engineer with the New Jersey telecommunications firm, was quite adept and original in translating the traditional Islamic attribute for God of "sustainer" into "evolver," and then parsing the meaning of evolution finely enough to accept macroevolution but reject microevolution ("monkey to man," as he said). In comparison, there was less innovation on more basic matters of the faith as they have been traditionally understood, particularly if they would challenge sacred texts and authorities. Even if religion and theology are self-taught and the holders of the monopoly of religious knowledge are distrusted or ignored by autodidacts, a certain degree of "preventive censorship by the institution is exerted without anyone having to apply controls and constraints" (Bourdieu 1984: 85). Autodidacts still expect the authorities (whether they be university, mosque, gudwara, or temple) to "indicate and open the short cuts of popularization and the vulgate, which are always, directly or indirectly, dominated by the institution," Bourdieu argues (85). In a wider context, Randall Collins (2005: 359) writes that because autodidacts tend to "build an intellectual identity upon . . . random access to cultural capital, [they are] unlikely to meet much success in the stratified networks that make up the intellectual world." Collins portrays such self-taught intellectuals as alienated, "individualistic and proud of it," and belligerent (in extreme cases and circumstances, even being numbered among serial killers and terrorists).

Although I will later argue that these professionals operate with more freedom than found in Bourdieu's portrayal and less alienation than suspected by Collins, it is the case that one's position in relation to the institution often determines the degree to which knowledge is accepted and dispersed. The necessity of maintaining contact with the networks surrounding the institution was recognized by most of the interviewees. This is vividly illustrated in the case of Rajiv, the retired computer science and management professor we met circulating among the book tables at his Hindu temple. He positioned himself as a critic of organized Hinduism and the way it appealed to the unenlightened rank-and-file and felt he did not need the guidance of priests, gurus, or swamis. Yet he remained a regular at the book counter at his temple, answering inquiries of—and sometimes arguing with—worshippers, and, returning to Bourdieu's framework, using the references and the lingo of traditional Hinduism, and even making a (unsuccessful) run for the temple's board of directors.

The professionals were autodidactic in their acquisition of scientific as well as religious knowledge. They tended, on one hand, to blur the line between their training and work in applied science and that of theoretical science in their claims to scientific knowledge. On the other hand, they frequently criticized the non-practical and tentative nature of theoretical science. Much of this criticism had religious undertones, holding that theoretical science unnecessarily and on scant evidence dismisses religious truth claims. Most were of the not wholly unwarranted opinion that theoretical scientists, particularly biologists, are not very religious in the traditional sense (Ecklund 2010).Yet they often used the findings of theoretical science to legitimize their claims that their respective religions had a special affinity for modem science. Their high valuation of science was applied to their religious lives, viewing their faiths as the "most scientific" and progressive. These patterns are also evident in accounts of immigrant Buddhist science professionals who translate their faith into scientific and rational terms, partly as an attempt to compete with the inroads of evangelical Christianity in their community (Chen 2008).

All of these believers often find themselves in the unsettling position of lauding the advances of theoretical science—from those in embryology to astronomy—in the cases when they confirmed their faiths while condemning this field and its methodology when its theories challenge their beliefs. To avoid this inconsistency, many adopted the idea of provisional science—that scientific theories are often speculative, incomplete, and even reversible. In this view, the believers' respective faith will be vindicated as the truth in the end so they need not take scientific challenges too seriously in the meantime. In fact, some took the next logical step, arguing that since science is such a changeable and unstable enterprise in the first place, it makes no sense and could even be self-defeating to seek scientific proofs for their teachings and beliefs.

The concept of provisional science is not limited to religious believers. The postmodern critique of science, stressing the situated and socially constructed nature of scientific work and theories, makes somewhat similar claims, even if it does not see any final resolution to the conundrum in the way that the believer does (Harding 1998).[2] In his critique of Muslim science, Taner Edis argues that both the conservative believer and the postmodernist distrust overarching theories that seek to explain away local knowledge (for the postmodernist) and supernatural beliefs (for the religious person). But in the believers' hands, the concept of provisional science means something quite different than relativism; the religious engineer and IT professionals I interviewed saw science as something universal that makes them modern, global, and American all at the same time. Provisional science serves to make religious beliefs plausible; miracles are still possible and divine revelation can reveal the "true" meanings to past, present, and future events. The frequent criticisms I heard of theoretical science were not always the result of a religious orientation; the conflict and rivalry between applied science and theoretical science have a long history (Noble 1977). But if theoretical science is provisional, at least in the eyes of these religious applied science professionals, then it is also of a somewhat lower status than applied science, which deals with the "real" world, producing tangible results that improve people's lives.

PRACTICAL RATIONALITY AND THE DE-TRADITIONALIZING OF RELIGION

The belief in the provisional nature of science and the value (in some cases even moral superiority) of practical over theoretical science for these professionals created a fertile field for the interaction between scientific and religious spheres. Even among non-believing scientists, such new technologies as artificial intelligence raises quasi-religious questions of meaning and the nature of human complexity (Unauthored 2006). The practical sciences built upon practices and concepts of order, design, and invention have a special affinity with the "strong theism" of the believing engineer or IT professional. Designing and then setting machine parts or software into action stirs up echoes of divine creation, order, and harmony, even the sense that one may be participating in such processes. That is one reason why many professionals from such disparate traditions as Islam, Hinduism, and Sikhism found Christian-based intelligent design theories (far more than simple and literal creationism) so appealing. Thus these applied scientists affirmed both (non-Darwinian) evolution and the existence of God through a concept originating within their own discipline; they had more difficulty accepting evolution outside of the framework of design, even though many theologians hold such a position (Miller 2007).

In one sense, of course, faith and values, not to mention matters of evolution and creation, are irrelevant to these fields; if the "work is done" and the "problems are solved," management and customers couldn't care less whether the engineer or software designer doing the work is an ardent atheist, pagan, or Mormon. But the meaning assigned to such work matters a good deal to the religious applied science professional. We saw this most clearly in the way the interviewees responded to my specific question about how they apply their faith to their work. Their answers were not so much about special insights they received from their respective faiths concerning engineering or designing software. Rather, they cited specific values and concerns generated by their faiths that they then applied to their work. These values and virtues impinged on the actual choices and manner in which several of these professionals conducted their work; they were not just private and internalized sentiments. This was most clearly illustrated by Krishna, the mechanical engineering professor who criticized the way theoretical science sees religious values as an intrusion and does not take responsibility for the consequences of its theories, while engineers would take precautions to ensure safer results, such as using material that is biodegradable.

The choice of which projects and positions to accept or reject was in several cases colored by these professionals' religious orientations. The Muslims, in particular, refused (or said they would refuse) work in security and defense that they feared might jeopardize their community, particularly in the wake of 9/11. As Ibrahim, the thirty-five-year-old computer science professor, said of his move away from defense work, "I began to see privacy as important, especially for Muslims. My faith moved me away from this direction. I began to see more fundamental issues [as important]." His concern about violating the rights of fellow Muslims moved him into the work of computer vision to aid visually impaired people.

One way in which the religious beliefs and perspectives informed these professionals' work was in the area of technology. The Muslim, Hindu, and Sikh applied science professionals for the most part displayed an optimism and easy acceptance of technological advances, even though there was some trepidation about approaching the frontiers of biotechnology, especially among the Muslims. The acceptance and admiration of technology might be expected among professionals who value such work not only for vocational reasons but also because of the immigrant desire for acceptance in a technological society. But the way in which technology was accepted and linked to societal progress often carried a religious dimension. Their more accepting attitudes were often compared with the stricter and "less scientific" views of American Christians. On more specific grounds, the Sikhs claimed the religious justification of divine destiny and the unfolding of God's will for their support of technological development.

But it is in the formation of values surrounding the motivation and attitudes involved in work where the religious factor was the strongest. It is also in this area where the particularities of Muslim, Hindu, and Sikh identities played a more apparent role in forming particular "work ethics." Most of the interviewees cited the general virtues of hard work, honesty, and fairness (and some were not sure that these virtues were directly related to their religious beliefs). But there was variation as to which virtues and values were highlighted by these professionals. The Hindus were the most likely to stress the personal spiritual impact of their faith on their work They tended to cite the spiritual practices (meditation) and teachings (karma and reincarnation) as giving them the strength and motivation to "do the right thing," such as being honest and hard-working. The Muslims also stressed hard work, but usually in the moral sense of reaching personal perfection—both in faith and vocation—which also extended to benevolence toward others. Tariq, the computer science professor at the business college, valued the human potential speaker Tony Robbins because of "his message that every day we should have some improvement is similar to the Islamic teaching of perfection."

The Sikhs were the most likely to stress what can be called the "social virtues," which would include tolerance, equality, sharing of wealth, and social justice. This was seen in the case of Ravindra, the civil engineer from New Jersey, who cited his father's company's generous health benefit plan as an example of how one's faith should influence one's work. That even the New Jersey computer programmer Ranjit, the most orthodox and unassimilated Sikh among the interviewees, stressed the social justice component as part of his work ethic suggests that integrating such values into one's job is not the result of diluting or secularizing the faith. In fact, such secularization could just as easily lead to a focus on materialist acquisition and calculated self-interest as to community-minded benevolence.

To return to the basic sociological line of reasoning employed at the beginning of this chapter, under modernity the individual draws on a repertoire of symbols, discourses, knowledge, virtues, practices, and beliefs from one or more (secular and religious) traditions in order to meet needs and provide meaning to a range of activities (from family life to occupation). Individuals select, internalize, and make these various elements their own, while the traditions also change and even mutate into new forms over time and in interaction with other traditions and spheres of life. Yet the repertoires or "genetic codes" of "religious logic" in these traditions are necessarily limited and tend in certain directions. The Muslim engineer, for instance, draws on a repertoire of exclusive devotion to the sacred text, and a striving for perfection that carries over into a tendency to "find" science in the Koran and to see one's career as a path of constant self-vigilance and self-improvement. The Hindu IT professional is likely to have been brought up under a constellation of habits, rituals, teachings, religious emotions, and experiences that move in the direction of spiritual and mental introspection with an undertone of ambivalence about a "worldly" life. It might be expected, therefore, that such professionals tended to weave spiritual and mystical exploration into scientific practices and speculation, and that the Hindu work ethic included an uneasy relation with wealth and success, perhaps suggested by the several interviewees' plans to pursue spiritual concerns full-time (and in India) in their retirement. To complete this exercise, the Sikh is presented from early life with both communal cohesion and with a suspicion of hierarchy and religious intermediaries. Throughout my interviews we saw how all of this translated into the Sikhs' maintaining a form of individualism that nevertheless stayed—however uneasily—within the bonds of the community. They were able to maintain a form of "inner-worldly" mysticism that serenely accepted the problems and promises of technological change.

But such "outworkings" of religious logic are far from the whole story. Understanding the religious discourses of these religious professionals is not just a matter of tracking sets of beliefs and practices as they are handed down from their original traditions and then applied to the modern world. Rather, once we understand the tradition-based underpinnings to such attitudes and behavior, we find that they have interacted with alternative religious and "socio-logics" and spheres of life, in some cases mutating into new forms of religious discourse. Under the influence of modernity and the therapeutic revolution, seeking spiritual perfection can easily mutate into the quest for self-help and therapeutic self-actualization—something that is appealing to not a few Muslims, as we saw in the cases of the civil engineer Shafiq and the computer science professor Tariq, who were involved in human potential groups. The Hindu spiritualization of science encounters the New Age movement and believers adopt its synthesis of science and spirituality as a way of legitimizing and popularizing what would otherwise be considered "foreign"concepts and teachings to Americans.

In fact, New Age, human potential, and alternative spiritualities have more than a passing similarity with the general disengagement toward tradition and religious authorities that was evident among many professionals. While it is not the case that most would spurn external revelations as expressed in the Vedas, the Koran, and the Guru Granth for internalized spiritual experiences in the way of a New Age seeker, there is some truth to the observation that many modern believers have taken a "subjective turn," playing the role of the seeker in relation to tradition. Paul Heelas and Linda Woodhead (2005) contrast what they call "life as religion," consisting of following external rules and authority passed down from a tradition with that of "subjective-life"spirituality concerned with inner-well-being and personal experience and authenticity. Such a process of "de-traditionalization" is far from recent and was similarly described by Durkheim a century ago as the difference between "a religion handed down by tradition" and a "free, private, optional religion, fashioned according to one's own needs and understanding" (cited in Pickering 1975: 96). What is noteworthy is that such a private religion in Durkheim's time was not very widespread, whereas Heelas and Woodhead and others (Houtman and Aupers 2007) report that it is becoming the norm, at least in much of contemporary Europe. That these detraditionalized sentiments are voiced by fairly recent immigrants from traditions outside of Western Christianity is a sign that such discourse is prevalent in the United States and that it is highly adaptable and appealing to other believers. Of course, Hinduism (and Sikhism, to a lesser extent) shares in the "holistic milieu," in the sense that it embraces practices (meditation and yoga) and spirituality (discovering the divinity within) that are on the menu of today's spiritual seeker.

As mentioned above, for the American Hindu, the New Age movement serves as a form of cultural capital from which they can draw to legitimize and spread their beliefs in the American religious marketplace. The circuitous route in which even newcomers to the United States "rediscover" traditional religion through non-traditional means was illustrated in the account of Sidha, a computer programmer who volunteered at the book counter at the Hindu temple. He was a nominal Hindu growing up in India and came close to losing his faith. He only discovered (or rediscovered) Hindu spirituality when he watched the New Age–oriented teachings of Wayne Dyer on PBS after he immigrated to the United States. It was his subsequent involvement with the Center for the Art of Living, a holistic-Eastern spiritual group including many non-Hindus, that defined and deepened his interest and involvement in Hinduism. The fact that Muslims, as well as Hindus and Sikhs, display some attraction to human potential-therapeutic techniques and teachings may be just as much related to the self-help and subjective values of upper-middle-class American corporate culture as to the mutations and affinities of their particular traditional beliefs (i.e., the Islamic ideal of striving for perfection and purity). The merging of an externally-driven Protestant work ethic with internalized motivational self-help and human potential techniques and teachings is a fact of the modem workplace. In many cases this development complements the specific practices of the professionals' religious traditions; a Muslim prayer room or space in an office is less conspicuous and offensive in firms which now commonly hold meditation retreats and have workplace chaplains (Miller 2007).

In discussing the religiosity of young adults, Robert Wuthnow (2007) finds that they engage in "spiritual tinkering." This is where available ideas, practices, and beliefs are pieced together "from the materials at hand," whether they come from partially recalled Sunday school lessons, conversations with friends, television programs, or websites. Wuthnow contrasts this

improvisational approach with "religious professionals who approach spirituality the way an engineer might construct a building." But I found that even
engineers do a significant amount of "tinkering" as they construct a religious
identity. Applied science provided the tools for these professionals to go on a
religious search, even if it was more often confined to the borders of their
respective religions rather encompassing the vast religious marketplace. Like
the spiritual seeker tinkering for available resources, these professionals did
not accept their traditions wholesale but rather applied the tools at hand,
those of practicality and empirical truth-seeking, as they constructed their
religious lives. These searches could move in "liberal" or "conservative"
directions. For the Hindu professional, applying the tools of practical rationality often meant a standardization of the religion, even though such an
outcome was expressed in very different ways. For the Muslim professional,
the applied science values of experimentation and empiricism often led
(though not always) to a subjective turn that moderated the objective demands of Islam as well as broadened out into a more pragmatic approach to
social and political matters.

As a religion between Hinduism and Islam, the Sikhs still relied on the
social capital of their communal bonds created by their distinct disciplines
(the 5 Ks), while individually choosing the most "essential" beliefs and practices, usually in accord with the modern ideals of social justice and equality.
A still-intact tradition protected by ethnic and language differences from the
wider American society made the Sikhs less likely to tinker and borrow from
other religions and spiritualities in building their identity (although that may
be changing among younger generations). It is an open question whether the
decline of such ethnic solidarity and increasing upward assimilation into the
American prosperous classes will also hasten de-traditionalization among the
Sikhs.

DIFFERENT RATIONALITIES OR RATIONALIZATION?

So far, I have argued that the religious discourse among the Muslim, Hindu,
and Sikh applied professionals is developed through a complex interplay of
occupational cultures and choices, institutions (universities, mosques, and
temples, as well as the structure and establishment of applied science in the
United States), traditions (both secular and religious), and, most important,
broader religious and social forces (such as de-traditionalization, immigration, and globalization). That such interactions between the rationalized discourses of applied science and other spheres and discourses are possible says
something important about rationality. The social scientific literature has
tended to portray work in the sciences and technology as leading if not to
secularization then to a "colonization" of religion by the alien logic of effi-

ciency, compartmentalization, standardization, and empiricism. To put it more simply, if work in science and technology does not make people godless, it is likely to make them fundamentalists. One reason for this simplification is due to the lack of in-depth research on the relation between scientists and religion. But the logic of the theory of rationalization as it has been proposed and developed in later sociology entails a deterministic—usually negative—impact on the vitality of religion rather than a more open-ended process of interaction.

For Weber, there are different kinds of rationality. The most obvious category of rationality that would apply to engineers and IT professionals is that of practical rationality. This is where everyday activity is ordered in a practical and efficient way, with the business-oriented strata in particular being the main carriers of this kind of rationality. Practical rationality would obviously encompass those in applied science, where the values of efficiency and standardization are thought to be equivalent to means-end strategies. Although they criticize some aspects of theoretical science, these professionals also exhibit the "theoretical rationality" elucidated by Weber in their embrace of logical deduction, empiricism and, most notably, the way they apply such logic to their own beliefs. Any attempt to apply conceptual thought to "non-rational" forms of life is an expression of theoretical rationality. In Weber's view, these forms of rationality (including the formal rationality of bureaucracies) increasingly invade other spheres of life, imposing their own logic. They particularly conflict with "substantive" rationality, which includes the values and traditions of religions and other ethical systems.

But Weber here is inconsistent regarding the effects of rationalization. On the one hand, he sometimes appears to make these other non-rationalized spheres very porous and fragile to the forces of rationality, while making the process of rationalization virtually immune from interaction with the non-rational, substantive spectrum, especially in his writings on science. On the other hand, Weber realized that substantive forms of rationality can influence and perhaps challenge practical rationality. Weber argued that both religious teachings and behavior could have their own effect on practical and formal rational domains. For instance, he attempted to show how sect membership interacted with and shaped the American credit system, even if such membership was eventually secularized and yielded to the forces of bureaucracy (Gerth and Mills 1946). Kahlberg (2005) argues that Weber nonetheless thought that these religion-influenced patterns of economic action can also endure in the form of civic values and ideals, at least in the context of the United States.

The key to understanding such apparent contradictions lies in Weber's comparative-historical approach. Even when he portrayed rationalization as advancing in a certain direction (toward the "iron cage," in the instance of capitalism), he did so in a particular historical and national context rather than as a process of universal and linear evolution. Kahlberg adds that the "power" of Weber's sociology is its ability "to combine large-scale model building ('modern Western rationalism') with ideal types, open-ended societal domains, social carrier groupings, and an emphasis on the multicausality of patterned social action and the intertwining of the present closely with the past" (Kahlberg 2005: 30–31).[3]

In the spirit, if not the letter, of Weber's approach, I argue that applied science is not as rational (in the sense of "practical rationality") and that religion is not as irrational and irrelevant as has been posited by classical and contemporary sociology. The heavy hand of practical rationality demanding efficiency, standardization, and compartmentalization (separating ethics and virtues from means-end strategies) can be altered through religious and other kinds of moral agency. In economist Deidre McCloskey's words, the values and "virtues" of "solidarity" and "temperance" may have a role in one's work in applied science (or finance) as much as the virtue of "prudence" (maximizing utility). McCloskey cites a study of the so-called rational estimates of costs for 258 big engineering projects between 1927 and 1998 which found overruns of 20 to 40 percent. The study found that the "entire structure of incentives is geared toward underestimating costs and overestimating benefits," incentives which could range from personal profit to aesthetic value (making a beautiful bridge) (McCloskey 2006: 435).

It can also be questioned how much the development of technology implies a corresponding growth of rationalization and the utilitarian values of efficiency and instrumentality. Erik Davis writes that "we often err in assuming that the cultural experience of tools and machines necessarily implies a strictly rational, reductive, or utilitarian worldview. Humanity has always built a technoculture, but only very recently (and fitfully) a scientific one. Human beings constructed, manipulated, and culturally engaged impressive tools and machines millennia before Enlightenment science arose to stamp out the old superstitions with what William Blake called its 'single vision'" (Davis 2005).

As the Hindu engineering professor Krishna noted, religious and ethical values find a home in applied science because both deal with the intended and unintended consequences of scientific developments; the natural sciences would more likely see imposing such values as "intruding" on its theorizing. The infusion of religion-based ethics and virtues, or substantive rationality, into the domain of practical rationality can be seen in the professionals' decisions and judgments about their work—for instance, whether to work in a specific project (such as involving the defense and intelligence agencies for Muslims after 9/11) that might be used to imperil their community or personal faith (such as gambling). The motivations and the meanings assigned to work, even if they were as simple and generic as honesty, hard work, and patience in the face of obstacles, were heavily influenced by faith commitments. The various work ethics I highlighted in the last section also channeled practical rationality into the desired and value-laden ends of achieving one's potential and spiritual purpose, altruism, and contemplation (and sometimes mimicking) of the divine.

To conclude this chapter, I have attempted to break down the amorphous concepts of religion and science into the specific groups, movements, and dynamics that make up the actual interactions between Muslim, Hindu, and Sikh professionals and applied science. I found that the similarities between these professionals are more important than their differences. They tend to share the turn to religious and scientific autodidacticism and individualism, while using science to legitimize their claims to modernity and an American identity. In other words, the forces of a specific immigration trajectory, mass education, and the applied science profession have significantly shaped the lives and discourse of these professionals. At the same time, these professionals belong to specific traditions with their own logics that particularly shape their work ethics and ways of dealing with the "world," and how they navigate the American (and, increasingly, global) religious marketplace. Because of the practical and flexible nature of applied science, these professionals are able to bring their religious identities to bear on their work in a unique way. But whether this new "knowledge class" can influence their own religious communities in an enduring way is a more difficult question that I will address in the concluding chapter.

NOTES

1. It might be expected that the discourse from the IT field would be somewhat different in both form and substance from that of engineering. The greater informality and decentralization of the IT working environment and education stands in contrast to the more traditional corporate and hierarchical structure of the engineering field. Today, however, there is a greater interplay between these two fields, largely because many IT professionals have engineering backgrounds, particularly those who were trained prior to the computer boom of the 1980s and 1990s, as well as because most fields of engineering draw on computer science. The link between these occupations was especially strong for the professionals I interviewed, as well as for many immigrant professionals in general who arrive in the United States from countries where engineering and computer science are not differentiated into two separate departments in universities. It is for these reasons that I did not find strong differences in the major aspects of religious discourse among the engineers and IT professionals.

2. My discussion about the constructed nature of the applied science professionals' discourse is in some ways similar to the postmodern constructivist position on science. As will be evident later in this chapter, I also agree that applied science is not the strictly utilitarian enterprise as some of its defenders and practitioners assert. However, I have more doubts about the relativist critique of theoretical science (deconstructing the content as well as the method of science), and I should stress that such a position is not implied in my argument about applied science.

3. It should be noted that my discussion of Weber and the different kinds of rationality is not meant to be an exhaustive or even cursory survey of the concept of rationality. I am concerned here with trying to account for the disparity between Weber's versatility in working

with the different kinds of rationality and his more rigid formulation of the secularizing force of science (practical and theoretical rationality) upon religion. I also deal with this dilemma in my discussion of secularization and science in the introduction, particularly focusing on the literature of the sociology of religion—for example, through the different approaches of Wuthnow (1985) and Smith (2003). Contemporary treatments of rationality found in the broader sociological literature have questioned the importance of means-end rationality and therefore can also be useful in rethinking the religion-science relationship. For instance, Habermas (1984: 85–94) distances himself from the concept that purposive-rational calculation is the last word regarding human behavior. Although not directly addressing science and religion, he introduces a complex concept of rationality and portrays modern society as differentiated into separate spheres, therefore producing different experiences.

Conclusion

Much of this book has demonstrated how work in technology and applied science is not necessarily a secularizing agent, but rather can be quite amenable to religious beliefs and practices. More important, I have found that professionals working in this field from various religions share a common religious-science discourse. For all their religious and cultural differences, they showed a high valuation of science and technology that supported their religious faiths even as they challenged and reshaped both orthodox scientific and religious concepts. As stated at the beginning of the previous chapter, it is their common immigrant and educational trajectories and patterns of integration into both the American professional class and religious market that provide the foundation on which this discourse is constructed. These professionals' greater ability to maintain transnational and globalized ties also contributed to the creation of this religio-scientific discourse.

Although I found it is doubtful that work and study in applied science have a uniform effect across cultures and religions, the practical rationality and pragmatism of these professions showed an affinity with the individualism and de-traditionalized nature of American and increasingly global religion. It may be the case that such a "scientific" religion may function in a way similar to that of civil religion—a generalized faith providing a bridge between specific beliefs and larger overarching meanings and morals in a technological age. Because of their common liminal positions, existing both in traditional and scientific cultures, the Muslim, Hindu, and Sikh engineers and IT professionals may be particularly adept in creating such a pan-religious-scientific discourse—a trend which may also apply to immigrant Buddhists and Orthodox Jews newly involved in technological fields (Chen 2008). Even while adhering to their respective religious authorities and sacred texts, these professionals insisted on formulating and thinking through their faiths in practical terms. The professionals' "mantra" of having "the most scientific religion" was often accompanied by the equally modem credo of "I'm more spiritual than religious." The fact that this discourse is shared by liberal Sikhs, spiritual and non-political Hindus, and relatively conservative Muslims suggests that it is distinct from a fundamentalist discourse.

I have sought to demonstrate how this common scientific-religious discourse is mediated by different traditions and interactions resulting in different outcomes and playing different functions, sometimes intentionally and strategically so. The Muslim religious and scientific discourse reveals a pragmatic turn that challenges a strictly ideological or Islamist reading of Islam. In other words, just because a Muslim engineer is conservative in his or her belief in the Koran does not necessarily translate into a corresponding conservatism or fundamentalism in the ways these beliefs are derived or applied to society. In fact, because Islam belief is arrived at through a process of searching and experimentation, it often leads to the conviction that others should come to Islam through a similar experiential and pragmatic manner in order to be "authentic."

In a way, the Hindu discourse spiritualizes both the religion and science, de-emphasizing the communal and ritual aspects of the faith while inserting a mystical and moral tone into scientific language and concepts. I try to show that there is a standardization and rationalization of Hinduism taking place, but that this change is also in tune with contemporary spirituality and its non-institutional and often practical expressions (seen in the interest in applying spirituality to work). So in this case also, I take issue with critics who associate high-tech Hindu professionals and fundamentalism. The Sikh discourse, even if it shares much with that of the Muslims and Hindus, seeks to differentiate Sikhism from Islam and Hinduism. These professionals tend to stress how Sikhism is peaceful, is tolerant, and promotes social justice, on one hand, and, on the other (and in response to perceptions of Hinduism), how it is egalitarian, non-hierarchical, and fully engaged in and compatible with science, technology, and society.

The preceding chapter sought to make the point both that the professionals' religious discourse is more scientific and open to practical rationality and that the applied science they practiced is more value-driven and less "rational" than is generally supposed. If that is the case, then both fields are likely to interact and influence each other. What might the implications be of such an interaction for the religious applied scientists and their faith communities?

For better or worse, this discourse arising from these interactions will likely find a place in these professionals' religious institutions; already, it is not difficult to find signs of such influence. These professionals form a "new knowledge class," not only because they can create and control new ideas for fellow believers, but because their work in the fields of knowledge and information lends them high status and power by American society

(Gouldner 1979). With their access to sophisticated technology and travel, these professionals can become, in Peggy Levitt's words, "global religious citizens," spreading their values and discourses to fellow believers around the world, not to mention to the countries of their origins. Some may not seek such citizenship, following older models as assimilated Americans or American ethnics (Levitt 2007). It appears that most of the professionals I interviewed (like many of America's new immigrants) occupy a place between total integration and transnational cosmopolitanism. But these professionals are the recipients of global currents that validate and enhance their status; their embrace of science, while maintaining religious and other kinds of transnational ties, is likely to be valued as much in their home countries as in the United States.

In fact, the applied science professionals' status in their own immigrant communities is somewhat more uncertain. Their autodidactic tendencies, seeking spiritual advice and assistance apart from traditional religious authorities, tend to leave them outside of the networks of influence that gather toward the center of religious institutions. Not having the community connections of doctors and businesspeople, the more isolated engineer or IT professional may have more influence on the Internet than at the temple or mosque. Further research is needed to determine how these professionals interact within their communities and families in ways that may extend or limit their influence.

Ironically, these professionals' proficiency in the American scientific culture may be both valued globally and met with indifference or even scorn by future (or present) generations who may also desire to know how their religious traditions relate to the arts, humanities, and social sciences. Already, the field of engineering, not to mention computer science, appears to be drawing less religious individuals—at least in the academic world—than such disciplines as nursing and finance (Gross and Simmons 2009). It may be the case that the affinity between technoscience and religiosity among American-born professionals will become less salient in the future. The belief that technological change is the will of God or that scientific logic is the best way to approach religious teachings is likely more problematic to Muslims, Hindus, and Sikhs who are untrained in the sciences. Although they may invoke justifications of technological progress from their respective religious traditions, applied science professionals may lack the necessary vocabulary to critique seemingly inevitable changes in technology that will influence society. Even for those working in technology, it may become apparent that the call for social justice and these religions' ethical dimensions in general become domesticated in the face of overwhelming acceptance of technological progress. The predominance of religio-scientific discourse may be moderated by increasing theological training in these traditions, as well as by exchanges and encounters with Christians, Jews, and secularists and the ways in which they have applied ethics to technological culture. The religious applied science professionals seem practical enough to listen to such demands and new voices to ensure their communities' continuing vitality.

LESSONS FROM THE EVANGELICAL TRAJECTORY

The relation between particular religious faiths and their vocational ethics, trajectories, and outcomes has been of interest to sociologists since Max Weber's pioneering work. The evangelicals in particular may be one segment of American religion where the relation between occupation and religious discourse and influence may be instructive to immigrant religious professionals and groups. Although few studies have been conducted on the involvement of evangelicals in business and applied science (including medicine), historical and anecdotal accounts have shown that these fields were very popular professions for these Christians, and that such laymen had significant influence in their churches and related organizations (Bruce 2002). Several leaders of the creationist movement come from the ranks of engineers, and businessmen such as Bill Bright put their indelible stamp on evangelicalism (Witham 2002).

Bright founded Campus Crusade for Christ, one of the most influential organizations in American evangelical history, and was largely known for his booklet "The Four Spiritual Laws," which outlined the plan of salvation in four easy steps. While evangelicals have always sought to present a simple message to reach the masses, these same Christians inherited confessions and creeds that were more comprehensive rather than formulaic. The Four Spiritual Laws can serve as a case study of how Christianity was further distilled and standardized according to sales techniques in order to reach a mass audience. In some sectors of evangelical Christianity, such as the New Christian Right and creationism, the involvement in applied science continues to the present. The business sector remains a receptive field for conversion and evangelism. But more recent studies have shown the emergence of a new evangelical elite in the media, arts, politics, and academia (Lindsay 2007). However, the standardized template laid down by Bill Bright and others from business and the practical sciences endures in evangelicalism, whether expressed in intelligent design, the entrepreneurialism of megachurches and the church growth movement, the "Purposeful Living" advice of Rick Warren, or just in the general ways of speaking and thinking among American evangelicals. At the same time, other discourses and ways of thinking have found a place in this many-layered movement, particularly the therapeutic mindset.

Throughout this study, we have seen many similar innovations among Muslim, Hindu, and Sikh applied science professionals—from a Hindu work ethic to pragmatic Muslim approaches to sharia, to Sikh technological optimism. As with the evangelicals, the forms of rationality, standardization, and pragmatism pioneered and popularized by the Muslim, Hindu, and Sikh applied science professionals will increasingly find a way into their religious communities.

References

Akyol, Mustafa. 2004. "Why Muslims Should Support Intelligent Design," IslamOnline.net, September 14, http://www.islamonline.net/english/Contemporary/2004/09/Article02.shtml, accessed May 3, 2006.

Amrute, Sareeta. 2010. "Living and Praying in the Code," *Anthropological Quarterly*, 83:3, 519–550.

Anderson, Jon W. 2005. "Wiring Up," in *Muslim Networks from Hajj to Hip Hop*, edited by Miriam Cooke and Bruce B. Lawrence (Chapel Hill: University of North Carolina Press).

Athar, Shahid. 1997. *Reflections of an American Muslim* (Chicago: KAZI Publications), 24, 221.

Batalova, Jeanne, and B. Lindsay Lowell. 2007. "Immigrant Professionals in the United States" *Society*, January/February, pp. 26–31.

Berger, Peter L., Brigitte Berger, and Hans Kellner. 1973. *The Homeless Mind* (New York: Random House), 25–40.

Berger, Peter L. 2012. "Further Thoughts on Religion and Modernity," *Society*, 49:4, 313–316.

Bourdieu, Pierre. 1984. *Distinction* (Cambridge: Harvard University Press).

Brant, Christa Case. 2014. "Israel's Newest Cyberwarriors: Ultra-Orthodox Jews," *Christian Science Monitor*, June 1, http://www.csmonitor.com.

Brown, C. Mackenzie. 2012. *Hindu Perspectives on Evolution* (London and New York: Routledge).

Brown, John K., Gary Lee Downey, and Maria Paula Diogo. 2009. "The Normativities of Engineers," *Technology and Culture*, 50:4, October, 737–752.

Bruce, Steve. 2002. *God is Dead: Secularization in the West* (Oxford: Blackwell Publishing), 106–117.

Bunt, Gary. 2003. *Islam in the Digital Age* (London: Pluto Press, 2003).

Burris, Val. 2001. "Small Business, Status Politics and the Social Base of New Christian Right Activism," in *Critical Sociology*, 27:1, 29–55.

Casanova, Jose. 2007. "Immigration and the New Religious Pluralism," in *Democracy and the New Religious Pluralism*, edited by Thomas Banchoff. (New York: Oxford University Press).

Chafri, Farida Faouzia. 2004. "When Galileo Meets Allah," in *New Perspectives Quarterly*, Fall, 118–123.

Chahal, Surjeet, Kaur. 2012. "Sikh Perspective on Modern Scientific Technology," in *Harmony in Science and Sikh Religion*, edited by S. H. Virk. (Mohali, India: Hardev Singh Virk), 114–126.

Chakravartty, Paula. 2000. "The Emigration of High Skilled Indian Workers to the United States: Flexible Citizenship and India's Information Economy," in *Working Paper 19*, August. The Center for Comparative Immigration Studies, University of California, San Diego.

Chen, Carolyn. 2008. *Getting Saved in America* (Princeton: Princeton University Press).

Collins, Randall. 2005. *Interaction Ritual Chains* (Princeton: Princeton University Press).

Connor, Phillip. 2007. "New Directions for Immigrant Religious Research," unpublished paper presented at the meeting of the Society for the Scientific Study of Religion, November 2–4, Tampa, Florida.

Constant, E. 1989. "Science, Society & Texas Petroleum Engineers," *Social Studies of Science*, 19:3, August, 439–472.

Cook, Michael. 2014. *Ancient Religions, Modern Politics* (Princeton: Princeton University Press).

Davis, Erik. 2005. "Reverse Imagineering: Technoculture and the Religious Imagination," in *The Future of Religion* (Stockholm: Axel and Margaret Axison Johnson Foundation, 2005), 51–62.

Durkheim, Emile.1965. *The Elementary Forms of Religious Life* (New York: The Free Press).

Eck, Diana. 2000. Negotiating Hindu Identities in the U.S.," in *The South Asian Diaspora in Britain, Canada, and the United States* (Albany: State University of New York Press).

Ecklund, Elaine Howard. 2010. *Science Versus Religion* (New York: Oxford University Press).

Edis, Taner. 2007. *An Illusion of Harmony* (Amherst, NY: Prometheus), 94–158.

Eikelman, Dale F., and Jon W. Anderson. 1999. *New Media in the Muslim World* (Bloomington, IN: Indiana University Press).

Esposito, John L. 2010. *The Future of Islam* (New York: Oxford University Press).

Evans, John H. 2002. *Playing God?* (Chicago: University of Chicago Press).

Evans, John H., and Michael S. Evans. 2008. "Religion and Science: Beyond the Epistemological Conflict Model," in *Annual Review of Sociology*, 34, 87–105

Everhart, Donald, and Salman Hameed. 2013. "Muslims and Evolution: A Study of Pakistani Physicians in the United States," in *Evolution: Education and Outreach*, 6:2, 1–8.

Gaffney, P.D. 1994. *The Prophet's Pulpit* (Berkeley: University of California Press).

Gambetta, Diego, and Steffen Hertog. 2009. "Why Are There So Many Engineers among Islamic Radicals?" in *European Journal of Sociology*, 50, 201–230.

Gerth, H. H., and C. Wright Mills, eds. 1946. *From Max Weber: Essays in Sociology* (New York: Oxford University Press).

Goodstein, Laurie. 2006. "U.S. Muslim Clerics Seek a Moderate Middle Ground," *New York Times*, June 18, 2006, at: http://www.nytimes.com/2006/06/18/us/18imams/html?_r=1&0ref=slogin, accessed May 14, 2007.

Gouldner, Alvin. 1979. *The Future of Intellectuals and the Rise of the New Class* (New York: Seabury).

Gross, Neil and Solon Simmons. 2009. "The Religiosity of American College and University Professors," in *Sociology of Religion*, Summer, 70:2, 101–129.

Gross, Neil. 2013. *Why Are Professors Liberal?* (Cambridge: Harvard University Press).

Harding, Sandra. 1998. *Is Science Multicultural?* (Bloomington: Indiana University Press).

Heelas, Paul, and Linda Woodhead. 2005. *The Spiritual Revolution* (Oxford: Blackwell Publishing).

Helweg, Arthur. 1999. "Transmitting and Regenerating Culture," in *Sikh Identity: Continuity and Change,* edited by N. Gerald Barrier and Pashaura Singh. (Manohar), 311.

Houtman, Dick, and Stef Aupers. 2007. "The Spiritual Turn and the Decline of Tradition: The Spread of Post-Christian Spirituality in 14 Western Countries, 1981-2000," *Journal for the Scientific Study of Religion*, 46:3, 305–320.

Huff, Toby. 1999. "Islam, Science and Globalization," Unpublished paper, Fall.

Jeldtoft, Nadia. 2010. "Islam as Lived: Ritualization, Authority and Individualization with Muslims in Denmark, Germany and the United States." Unpublished paper presented at Center for the Study of New Religions (CESNUR) conference, Torino, Italy, September, 9–11.

Khan, Muqtedar. 2002. *American Muslims* (Beltsville, MD: Amana Publications), 118–120.

Kahlberg, Stephen, ed. 2005. *Max Weber: Readings and Commentary on Modernity* (Oxford: Blackwell), 27–32.

Keefe, Jeffrey, and Denise Potosky. 1997. "Technical Dissonance: Conflicting Portraits of Technicians," in *Between Craft and Science*, edited by Stephen Barley and Julian Orr (Ithaca: Cornell University Press), 53–81.

Kumar, J. A. 2005. "Highlights of Hi-Faith," at: http://www.boloji.com/opinion/0119.htm

Kurien, Prema. 2007. *A Place at the Table* (New Brunswick: Rutgers University Press).

Leonard, Karen. 2003. *Muslims in the U.S.: The State of Research* (New York: Russell Sage Foundation).

Lessinger, Joanna. 2001. "Class, Race and Success: Two Generations of Indian-Americans Confront Their Dream," in *Migration, Transnationalism and Race in a Changing New York*, edited by Robert Smith et al. (Philadelphia: Temple University Press, 2001), 6–11.

Levitt, Peggy. 2007. *God Needs No Passport* (New York: The New Press).

Lindsay, Michael. 2007. *Faith in the Halls of Power* (New York: Oxford University Press).

Lofti, Abudul, Hamid. 2002. "Spreading the Word: Communicating Islam in America," in *Muslim Minorities in the West*, edited by Yvonne Haddad, and Jane Smith (Walnut Creek, CA: Alta Mira Press) 160–177.

Mann, Gurinder Singh. 2006. "Making Home Abroad: Sikhs in the United States," in *A Nation of Religions*, edited by Stephen Prothero. (Chapel Hill, NC: University of North Carolina Press), 160–177.

Martin, David. 2002. *Christian Language and its Mutations* (Hants, UK: Ashgate), 33–42.

———. 2005. *On Secularization* (Hants, UK: Ashgate).

Mathew, Bijou, and Vijay Prashad. 2000. "The Protean Forms of Yankee Hindutva," in *Ethnic and Racial Studies*, 23:3, May, 516–534.

McCloskey, Deidre. 2006. *The Bourgeois Virtues* (Chicago: University of Chicago Press).

McLeod, W. H. 2001. *Exploring Sikhism* (New York: Oxford University Press), 162–186.

Merton, Robert. 1962. "Puritanism, Pietism, and Science," in *the Sociology of Science* (New York: The Free Press), edited by Bernard Barber and Walter Hirsch, 33–66.

Merton, Robert K. 1995. "The Thomas Theorem and The Matthew Effect." In *Social Forces*, December, 74(2): 379–424.

Miller, David. 2007. *God at Work* (New York: Oxford University Press).

Miller, Kenneth. 2007. "Faulty Design," in *Commonweal*, October 12, 31–33.

Nanda, Meera. 2003. *Prophets Facing Backwards* (New Brunswick, NJ: Rutgers University Press).

Noble, David. 1977. *America by Design* (New York: Knopf), 3–49.

Norris, Pippa, and Ronald Inglehart. 2004. *Sacred and Secular* (Cambridge: Cambridge University Press).

Oberoi, Harjot. 1994. *Construction of Religious Boundaries* (Chicago: University of Chicago Press).

Pace, Enzo. 2006. "The Inner-Worldly Mysticism and Successful Social Integration of the Sikh Panth in Italy." Unpublished paper presented at the annual meeting of the Association for the Sociology of Religion, Montreal, August 10–12.

Pew Research Center. 2006. *Muslim Americans* (Washington: Pew Research Center), 2–15.

Pickering, W.S.F. 1975. *Durkheim on Religion* (London: Routledge and Keegan Paul).

Prakesh, Gyan. 1999. *Another Reason: Science and the Imagination of Modern India* (Princeton: Princeton University Press).

Rainier. 2006. "The Quaran Predicts the Usage of the Element 'Aordium,'" *Islam.com*, December 26, at: http://www.islam.com/reply.asp?id=863034&ct=2&mn=863034, accessed: March 6, 2007.

Rajaee, Farhang. 1993. "Islam and Modernity: The Reconstruction of an Alternative Shi'ite Islamic Worldview in Iran," in *Fundamentalisms and Society*, edited by Martin E. Marty and R. Scott Appleby. (Chicago: University of Chicago Press), 103–125.

Rajagopal, Arun. 2000. "Hindu Nationalism in the U.S.," *Racial and Ethnic Studies*, Vol. 23, No. 3, May, 467–496.

Rao, N. N. 2005. "'Workship' with Grattitude," *Hinduism Today*, October/December.

Riesebrodt, Martin. 1993. *Pious Passion* (Chicago: University of Chicago Press).

Roy, Olivier. 2004. *Globalized Islam* (New York: Columbia University Press).

———. 1994. *The Failure of Political Islam* (Cambridge: Harvard University Press, 1994), 90–106.

Sachdev, Chhavi. 2006. "A Pragmatic Culture," in *Science & Theology News*, March, 24–25.

Shanavas, T. O. 2005. *Creation AND/OR Evolution: An Islamic Perspective* (New York: Xlibris).

Shapiro, Samantha M. 2006. "Ministering to the Upwardly Mobile Muslim," *The New York Times Magazine*, April 30.

Sidhu, G. S. 2003. *Science and Sikhism* (London: FIL), downloaded December 12, 2007 at: http://www.wellington.net.nz/Sikh_Religion.pdf.

Sikhism FAQs. 2007. "What is the Microcosmic Theory in Sikhism?" downloaded September 12 at: hhttp://www.allaoboutsikhs.com/faqs/sikhism-faqs-what-is-the-microcosmic-theory-in-sikhism.

Singh, Bhupinder. 2014. "The Five Symbols of Sikhism" in *Sikh Formations*, 10:1, 105–172.

Singh, Harsimran. 1998. *The Divine Truth* (Glen Cove, NY: Divine Power).

Singh, I. J. 2012. "Science Versus Religion: What Conflict?" in *Harmony in Science and Sikh Religion*, edited by S. H. Virk. (Mohali, India: Hardev Singh Virk), 150–157.

Sippy, Shana. 2005. "Hindutva in Northern California," unpublished paper presented at the annual meetings of the American Academy of Religion, November, Philadelphia.

Sivan, Emmanuel. 1985. *Radical Islam: Medieval Theology and Radical Politics* (New Haven: Yale University Press), 80, 118–119.

Smith, Christian. 2003. *The Secular Revolution* (Berkeley: University of California Press).

Stenberg, Leif. 1996. *Islamization of Science* (Lund, Sweden: Novapress).

———. 2000. "Science in the Service of God," in *ISIM Newsletter*, June, 11.

Suyuti. 2007. "Islam on Communications Technology," *Islam.com*, January 9, at: http://www.islam.com/reply.asp?id=868361&ct=2&mn=868361, accessed October 11, 2007.

Thornton, Patricia. "A Sociology of Entrepreneurship," in *Annual Review of Sociology*, Vol. 1, No. 25, 19–46.

Thornton, Patricia and William Ocasio. 2008. "Institutional Logics,"in *Sage Handbook of Organizational Institutionalism*, edited by Roystan Greenwood, Christine Oliver, Kerstin Sahlin, and Roy Suddaby. (Thousand Oaks: Sage).

Tibi, Bassam. 1993. "The Worldview of Sunni Arab Fundamentalists: Attitudes toward Modern Science and Technology," in *Fundamentalisms and Society*, edited by Martin Marty, and R. Scott Appleby. (Chicago: University of Chicago Press), 73–102.

Tulasi, Srinivas. 2002. "A Tryst with Destiny," in *Many Globalizations*, edited by Peter L. Berger, et al. (New York: Oxford University Press), 89–116.

Unauthored. 2006. "Resistance is Futile," in *What is Enlightenment?* September–December, 26.

Van der Veer, Peter. 2005. "Virtual India: Indian IT Labor and the Nation-State," in *Sovereign Bodies*, edited by Thomas B. Hanson. (Princeton, NJ: Princeton University Press).

———. 2014. *The Modern Spirit of Asia* (Princeton, NJ: Princeton University Press).

Varisco, Daniel Martin. 2010. "Muslims and the Media in the Blogsphere," *Contemporary Islam*, 4: 157–177.

Vaughan, Ted. R., Douglas H. Smith, and Gideon Sjoberg. 1966. "The Religious Orientations of Natural Scientists," in *Social Forces*, Vol. 44, No. 4, June, 519–526.

Veylanswami, Satguru. 2007. "What is Hinduism?" in *Hinduism Today*, January/March.

Virk, S. H., ed. 2012. *Harmony in Science and Sikh Religion* (Mohali, India: Hardev Singh Virk).

Weber, Max. 1978. *Economy and Society*, Vol. 1, edited by G. Roth and C. Wittich. (Berkeley: University of California Press).

Wilensky, Harold L., and Jack Ladinsky. 1967. "From Religious Community to Occupational Group: Structural Assimilation among Professors, Lawyers, and Engineers," in the *American Sociological Review*, Vol. 32, No. 4, August, 541–561.

Williams, Raymond Brady. 1998. "Asian Indian and Pakistani Religions in the United States," in *Annals of the American Academy of Political and Social Science*, 558, July, 178–195.

Wilson, Bryan. 1982. *Religion in Sociological Perspective* (New York: Oxford University Press), 54–57.

Witham, Larry. 2002. *Where Darwin Meets the Bible* (New York: Oxford University Press).

Wuthnow, Robert. 2007. *After the Baby Boomers* (Princeton: Princeton University Press).

———. 2005. "Science and the Sacred" in *The Sacred in a Secular Age,* edited by Phillip Hammond. (Berkeley: University of California Press), 187–203.

Zaidman, N. 2000. "The Integration of Indian Immigrants to Temples Run by North Americans," in *Social Compass*, 47: 2, 219.

Zinsmeister, Karl. 2005. "Case Closed," in *American Enterprise*, January/February, 42–45.

Index

About the Author

Richard Cimino is founding editor of *Religion Watch*, a monthly publication reporting on trends and research in contemporary religion. He currently teaches sociology at the University of Richmond in Virginia and is the author and coauthor of several books, including *Atheist Awakening*, *Trusting the Spirit*, and *Shopping for Faith*.

CPSIA information can be obtained at www.ICGtesting.com
Printed in the USA
BVOW07*1613020914